M000201480

REGIONAL
SETTLEMENT
DEMOGRAPHY IN
ARCHAEOLOGY

PRINCIPLES OF ARCHAEOLOGY

ADVISORY EDITORS

Robert L. Bettinger, *University of California, Davis*
Gary M. Feinman, *The Field Museum, Chicago, Illinois*

A PRIMER ON MODERN–WORLD ARCHAEOLOGY
Charles E. Orser, Jr.

REGIONAL SETTLEMENT DEMOGRAPHY IN ARCHAEOLOGY
Robert D. Drennan, C. Adam Berrey, Christian E. Peterson

REGIONAL SETTLEMENT DEMOGRAPHY IN ARCHAEOLOGY

Robert D. Drennan
University of Pittsburgh, Pittsburgh, Pennsylvania

C. Adam Berrey
University of Pittsburgh, Pittsburgh, Pennsylvania

Christian E. Peterson
University of Hawai'i at Mānoa, Honolulu, Hawai'i

ELIOT WERNER PUBLICATIONS, INC.
CLINTON CORNERS, NEW YORK

Library of Congress Cataloging-in-Publication Data

Drennan, Robert D.
Regional settlement demography in archaeology / Robert D. Drennan
and C. Adam Berrey, University of Pittsburgh, Pittsburgh, Pennsylvania,
Christian E. Peterson, University of Hawaii at Manoa.
pages cm. – (Principles of archaeology)
ISBN 978-0-9898249-4-1 – ISBN 0-9898249-4-2
1. Land settlement patterns, Prehistoric. 2. Archaeology – Methodology. I.
Berrey, C. Adam. II. Peterson, Christian E. III. Title.
GN799.S43D74 2015
930.1 – dc23

2014043484

ISBN-10: 0-9898249-4-2
ISBN-13: 978-0-9898249-4-1

Copyright © 2015 Eliot Werner Publications, Inc.
PO Box 268, Clinton Corners, New York 12514
http://www.eliotwerner.com

All rights reserved

No part of this book may be reproduced, stored in a retrieval system,
or transmitted in any form or by any means, electronic, mechanical,
photocopying, microfilming, recording, or otherwise, without
written permission from the Publisher.

Printed in the United States of America

PREFACE

This book began in a convergence of several observations. First, as we argue in Chapter 1, all regional settlement analysis is built on a demographic foundation in that it informs us about ancient societies by identifying patterns in how many people lived (and did other things) where. The patterns of how many people live and do other things where are the quintessential subject matter of demography. Second, regional settlement analysis is held back when its demographic foundation is not recognized explicitly (and often it is not). Third, archaeological surveys often use field methods that are less than optimal for collecting the data needed to build the demographic foundation for regional settlement analysis. Fourth, the whole subject of demography in archaeology is frequently met with skepticism if not outright hostility. Fifth, much of this reaction can be attributed to ignorance or misunderstanding of the field and analytical methods that represent best practices in regional demography in archaeology. (We thank reviewers of articles and grant proposals over the years for continual reminders of this ignorance and misunderstanding.) Sixth, this state of affairs is attributable in part to the fragmentation of essential methodological discussion in widely scattered primary reports of field research in different parts of the world that specialists in other regions seldom know about, much less read.

The aim of this book, then, is to pull together into a single, coherent account the basic methods of regional settlement demography, beginning at square one. It is not a literature review, so there are no citations in the text. The sources of data for examples are credited in a bibliography at the end of the book, and suggestions for further reading at the end of each major chapter lead to relevant references (listed in the same order as the topics they relate to in the chapter text). We have drawn very heavily on our own experience of regional settlement survey in the field and demographic analysis of data we have collected—not because our own work is so much more important than other projects, but because it is our own experience that has shaped our perspective; because this experience is a ready source of examples of the principles we try to make clear; and because the full, detailed datasets we work with in the book are most readily available to us from our own research. We express our appreciation to the entities that have funded this research, principally the U.S. National Science Foundation, and we are deeply grateful to literally hundreds of colleagues and students of more than a dozen nationalities with whom we have shared the experience of carrying out this research on three continents. Without their hard work and probing questions, this book could not have been born.

We attempt to outline here what we regard as best practices for regional settlement demography. We know that not everyone agrees about just what best practices are, so we have tried to provide the reasons behind our judgments, and we sometimes use comparative examples to show why we think some practices work better than others. Discussion of practices that have not worked out as well as anticipated helps us learn from our mistakes—and mistakes we have made ourselves are included. Our hope is to end every research project knowing how to do it better next time.

The methods and their implications are sometimes complicated. Regional settlement demography for ancient populations is a complicated challenge, one that can only be met successfully by avoiding simplistic assumptions and developing complex and powerful methodologies. Carrying out convincing demographic analysis in archaeology requires mastery of these methods and thorough understanding of their principles. Our hope is that we can open the door to these methods and principles by starting at the beginning and putting together the important elements of the story in a compact, integrated, coherent, and clear account. The beginning, for us, is not field methods. We start instead with a consideration of what regional settlement demography can tell us, and continue by considering how we can extract this information from things we can observe in the archaeological record. The intricacies of methods for collecting data in the field come where they belong: at the end. It is only by first sorting out what we will do with the data once they're collected that we can hope finally to separate the methodological sheep from the goats.

CONTENTS

CHAPTER 1

REGIONAL SETTLEMENT DEMOGRAPHY: WHY BOTHER?

Archaeologists have often considered making population estimates for prehistoric periods a highly risky, if not impossible, endeavor. Determining the number of people who left a particular set of archaeological remains is indeed complicated and the result is almost inevitably very approximate. It is well worth asking why we should even bother to try.

The simple answer is that we can't avoid it—at least not if our aims go beyond mere description of the ancient things that we find to consideration of the people who made them and the communities they lived in. Much human action is, in fact, *inter*action with other people, and these webs of varied kinds of interaction comprise the units of society at a range of scales. In this context people are, well, a population, and populations are what demography is about.

In very fundamental ways, people's actions and interactions are facilitated and constrained differently in interacting populations of different characters and sizes. This is not a novel observation. It is fully encapsulated in jokes about small towns where everyone knows everyone else's business and in clichés about the anonymity of the big city. Demographic analysis includes not only counting the number of people in a place, but also assessing other characteristics of populations. For regional settlement demography in archaeology, the spatial distributions of people and their activities loom especially large—but any successful effort to comprehend human social organization must take cognizance of the size and other characteristics of the population that is organized.

Since its beginnings in the mid-20th century, regional settlement study in archaeology has had demography at its core, with strong and explicit emphasis on the size and spatial distribution of populations. Gordon Willey is usually considered the founder of regional settlement archaeology, but the 450-page report of his landmark Virú Valley project of the 1940s dedicates barely five pages to population and something less than that to sociopolitical organization. The concluding 22-page chapter of the report focuses on comparing not the populations or societies of the Virú Valley with those of other parts of Peru, but on comparing the material archaeological remains themselves.

The concepts and methods of regional settlement archaeology, fully recognizing the core importance of demography, owe much more to the work of William Sanders and Jeffrey Parsons in the Basin of Mexico in the 1960s and 1970s. Sanders described the Basin of Mexico project as an effort to apply Willey's methodology, but in fact four years of methodological experimentation and innovation were required to develop the methods used in the Basin of Mexico, which in the end bore little resemblance to Willey's. The work of Sanders, Parsons, and their colleagues in the Basin of Mexico is really where the path starts that leads to the approaches we discuss in this book.

Sanders and his colleagues argued strongly that population growth and population pressure were major forces causing long-term economic, social, and political change, and a central aim of the Basin of Mexico settlement project was to collect empirical information to support this argument. This has contributed to a widespread misconception that efforts to study ancient demography in general are similarly motivated. While Sanders and others have indeed interpreted the results of their Basin of Mexico research as supporting a major causal role for population pressure, a number of other researchers (including the authors of this book) have argued precisely the opposite—also basing our conclusions on the results of the Basin of Mexico project. The disagreement is not about Sanders and colleagues' account of how many people lived where in the Basin of Mexico and how this changed through time. It is about the implications these demographic findings have for our understanding of the dynamics of social change.

It is logical that those who think population pressure is an important force for social change should be interested in ancient demography. It is also logical that those hoping for empirical evidence against this proposition should be interested in ancient demography. This idea is indeed one reason why we should bother with regional settlement demography. It is not true in general, however, that archaeologists dealing with demographic issues think that population *pressure* matters much (or at all). There are much broader and more fundamental reasons why we should bother with regional demography.

PEOPLE IN LANDSCAPES

How a population distributes itself across a landscape is obviously related to material issues like resource use. Settled farming populations are likely to live relatively close to the land they cultivate. This may involve shifting residence seasonally to cultivate in multiple locations. Hunting, gathering, or herding populations may reduce daily commuting time (which could often reach entirely unsustainable levels) by shifting residence locations on a scale of days, weeks, or months. Proximity to raw material sources of many different kinds is among the factors considered by craft producers in deciding where to live. Assessing spatial associations between resource locations and residence locations has long been a staple of regional settlement analysis. Interpreting the associations that may be observed involves least-effort transportation principles in the form of an assumed desire on the part of the inhabitants of a landscape to reside relatively close to places where they must frequently be, in order to exploit the resources they depend on for survival.

Analytical use of this truism has sometimes been taken for an assertion that economic concerns determine residence locations, but this does not follow. Least-effort transportation principles simply imply that residence locations are likely to be relatively close to places where people must be frequently (or *want* to be frequently) for any kind of reason. For any individual or household, there will be forces pulling in conflicting directions over the choice of residence location. Resource locations and other material or economic concerns like those just mentioned will almost certainly be among them, but so will non-material concerns like participation in religious ritual at certain locations and the simple pleasure of social interaction with neighbors (or its evil twin, avoidance of conflicts with neighbors). Sometimes people don't distribute themselves across a landscape in the most economically rational form for, say, subsistence production. This means that other forces have overridden such straightforward survival concerns, and such an observation opens a door for the investigation of other aspects of people's lives that are usually harder to get at with archaeological evidence. In such cases regional settlement demography yields information about subjects like religious or political organization.

"Agency" joined the fashionable buzzwords of archaeology at the turn of the 21st century. It has come to mean many different things, but it is sometimes the standard bearer for individual freedom to act and is set in contrast to the macroanalyses of regional settlement study. The demographic scale and organization of communities are nonetheless essential features of the contexts in which agents pursue their aims. The actions people take are facilitated, channeled, or constrained by demographic parameters (among other things, of course). Strategies of action that may be successful in a village of 500 may have no impact at all in a town of 5,000.

Beyond simple numbers, the spatial characteristics of a population matter. The strategy of action that succeeds in a village of 500 may fail in a looser community of 500 dispersed in 100 widely separated family farmsteads. These fundamental demographic parameters of scale and spatial distribution, then, and agents' perceptions of them are involved both in people's decisions about what actions to take and in determining the outcomes of those actions (which may or may not be what the actors anticipated).

At perhaps the opposite extreme of concepts of agency is agent-based modeling, in which individual agents are ordinarily presumed not to act in the idiosyncratic ways prized by some advocates of the notion of agency. Agent-based models commonly produce trajectories of changing distributions of population across a landscape. Evaluation of the utility of the models centers on comparing these trajectories with those that actually occurred across time in the past, as revealed by archaeological evidence. Regional settlement demography, then, provides critical empirical evidence for the validation of agent-based models.

Archaeological study of the size and spatial characteristics of populations has sometimes been cast in opposition to perspectives that are more mentalist than materialist. Landscape archaeology is sometimes posed in this way as a perspective in conflict with regional settlement demography. Sometimes this is simply a failure to recognize that regional settlement archaeology, properly done, has *always* been an investigation of people and landscapes. (Unsystematic prospecting for archaeological sites with little consideration of either landscapes or people does not comprise regional settlement archaeology, properly done.) In the realm of landscape archaeology, it is common to emphasize that landscapes are not purely natural phenomena but products of interaction between humans and the natural environment, and to use phrases like "landscapes of power" or "landscapes of memory."

At its most extreme, landscape archaeology can focus on what it must have felt like for, say, a Neolithic person to stand in a particular landscape and look around, and such efforts are usually thought to be far removed from demography. But surely the knowledge of who lived, was buried, farmed, prayed, partied, or made excellent stone axes where in that landscape would have played a large part in shaping the feelings of that Neolithic person standing there. So would the knowledge that no one lived on or even dared climb that hill over to the northwest because of the evil power that lurked in its forests. These are the characteristics of populations and population distribution that regional settlement demography gives us a means to estimate. A landscape archaeology without these elements has omitted the human part of the human : natural interaction that produces a landscape (or, worse yet, substituted the subjective intuitions of the modern archaeologist for the ancient human part). Landscapes of power and landscapes of memory involve more than just monuments and archaeologists.

There are, then, quite a lot of highly varied reasons to bother with regional settlement demography. In fact, archaeologists have been in the business of settlement demography ever since the first of our tribe returned excitedly from the field with news of finding a great site to dig. It was an exceptionally large site with an extremely high density and variety of artifacts and the obvious remains of large-scale architecture of several kinds. It was definitely worth putting a shovel into—so much to be learned about the important and powerful people who lived at this large and impressive regional capital and center of innovation.

The gist of this thinking about what makes great sites to dig is very much still with us, and regional settlement demography figures prominently among its implicit assumptions (both theoretical and methodological). Theoretically, it takes for granted the notion that very complex societies will likely have one or more settlements with especially large populations, including the most important people; that a wide variety of activities will be carried on at these large settlements; and that residents of smaller, less impressive settlements will be drawn to these "central places" for their special facilities and activities. Methodologically, this thinking takes for granted that such places will show up in the archaeological record as spatially extensive areas where highly varied artifacts can be found in large numbers and the remains of monumental-scale architecture may well be preserved. These notions are demographic: they're about the size and spatial organization of populations and their activities. These are the notions that have traditionally underlain archaeologists' decisions about where to dig, although they usually remain unspoken in that context.

BEST PRACTICES

Even archaeologists who staunchly resist making population estimates are likely to harbor deeply held (if very approximate) convictions about how many people lived at the settlements they investigate. Tell a Mesoamericanist excavating an initial Formative village that you think it had 5,000 residents, or remark to the excavator of a Longshan walled town with remains of a palace that you think its population was less than 1,000, and you'll be quickly challenged. The choice, then, is not whether to engage in regional settlement demography or not. We've been in it up to our ears for generations. The choice is whether to deal with demographic issues implicitly and subjectively, with no attention to methodology, or to pay explicit attention to demography and hone the relevant methodological tools to the sharpest possible edge.

This book is for those who choose the second option. It is concerned with what we regard as best practices in regional settlement demography in archaeology. For us the task of regional settlement demography is to assess how many people lived (and did other things) where in a region. Since the context is archaeology, it goes without saying that this extends to how these patterns changed through time—long spans of time.

Demographic analysis is carried out at a wide range of scales, and region has meant very different things to different archaeologists (Figure 1.1). When we use the word "region" here, we are usually thinking of areas of 100 km^2 or more—sometimes up to several thousand km^2. A region is bigger than a locality and is likely to include a number of separate local communities or settlements. A region is not generally as large as a nation or even a province, though, because it is not usually within our reach to collect archaeological data suitable for much demographic analysis at such large geographic scales. Regional-scale settlement demography is often built on a foundation of detailed information for much smaller scales, such as single settlements or local communities or even single households. We will thus consider demographic analysis at these smaller scales, but the emphasis will be on elements that help us scale the analysis up to entire regions.

We will not deal here with bioarchaeological approaches to the demographic analysis of burial populations, which is what archaeologists usually have in mind when they use the word "paleodemography." These bioarchaeological methods are especially good at detecting episodes of demographic growth and decline in cemeteries that are then taken to represent their region and/or period. Paleodemography in the bioarchaeological sense provides an important complement to regional settlement demography, but regional settlement demography is a much more direct approach to the questions of how many people there were in a region and how they distributed their residences and other activities across the landscape.

Regional settlement demography provides especially potent tools for comparative investigation. In numbers of people and in patterns of distribution, it finds a common abstract language for characterizing and discussing both similarities and differences between different periods and different regions. These patterns relate to social, political, economic, and religious organization and thus help us observe more acutely how the peoples of different regions organized their affairs in similar or varied ways. When these patterns are traced diachronically, they make it possible to lay entire trajectories of social change alongside each other to assess their similarities and differences. We cannot pretend to deal with all aspects of regional settlement demography in this small book; our selection is strongly slanted in the direction of methods that are especially helpful for working toward such comparative goals.

It is superficially appealing to insist on rigid application of the exact same methods in different regions in order to arrive at comparable results. It turns out, however, that methodological rigor and flexibility are more useful than rigid consistency. Concern for comparability of results is by no means misplaced, but the nature of the archaeological record varies enormously from place to place. Paradoxically, the methods applied to differ-

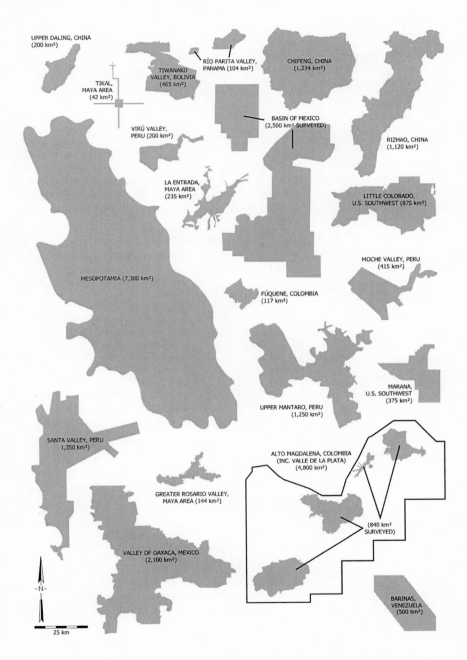

Figure 1.1. The boundaries of some well-known regional settlement studies, drawn to the same scale.

ent regions must often be different in order to produce comparable results. Rigidly consistent application of methods that produce reliable accounts of how many people lived where in one region are virtually guaranteed to produce unreliable and certainly non-comparable accounts for other regions where environment, ancient ways of life, and the nature of the archaeological record are different.

There is thus no single rigidly prescribed "right" way to do regional settlement demography in archaeology. It does not follow from this, however, that there is no "wrong" way. Like any other task, regional settlement demography can be done well or badly. Good approaches to regional settlement demography are designed to answer explicitly articulated research questions; their methods are carefully thought out logically and are as well supported empirically as possible. To some extent the articulation of research questions, the logical mapping out of methods, and the provision of empirical support for the validity of the methods are transferable from one region to another—as long as such transfers are made with careful skeptical attention to their logical and empirical appropriateness.

These are the complex methodological issues subsequent chapters will consider. In those chapters we will present what have become relatively standard approaches in regional settlement demography, as well as more recent and less familiar innovations, and we will try to open doors to continuing improvement in methods of regional settlement demography in the future. We defer the issue of data collection in the field until the last chapter, even though data collection must obviously precede analysis. This is because the rationale for collecting data in particular ways depends entirely on what sorts of subsequent analysis those data must be capable of sustaining. In research design consideration of analytical approaches must precede the determination of data collection techniques, and this book follows that plan.

APPROXIMATION

One final—and essential—point must be made before going on to those chapters. Regional demographic approximations in archaeology are just that: approximations. When archaeologists talk about the number of inhabitants in a place in either absolute ("500 people") or relative ("twice as many people") terms, these *must* be taken as very approximate characterizations. The same is true of statements about patterns in a population's spatial distribution, the distribution within the population and across space of various kinds of activities, and other broadly demographic conclusions.

In this, archaeologists engaging in regional demographic analysis are in the same boat as census analysts (with whom we share a great deal more as well). Counts of modern populations seem so much easier than counts of archaeological populations, but both are notoriously approximate. One reason is that counts of large numbers of things are always subject to at least small errors. Each hotly contested election demonstrates yet again that every time you count the ballots you will come up with a different total. Every census in the world recognizes that in addition to such random errors, there is bias in population counts. Some sectors of any population are easier to count than others, for a number of different reasons. Some of the approaches considered later in this book to assessing how precise our archaeological estimates are, and how we might make them more precise, are inspired by practices that have become standard in census taking.

Finally, though, it is imperative to recognize that regional demography—both modern and ancient—is not like banking. We expect more of our bankers than a rough estimate of the amount of money in our accounts. Census takers and archaeological demographers, however, cannot aspire to much more than rough estimates. It will sometimes be the case that these estimates are not precise enough to answer our questions with very much confidence, and we must be able to recognize when we are in this territory so as not to make dubious conclusions but try to achieve greater precision instead. But it will often be the case that the rough estimates we are able to make provide a sound basis for answering the questions we need to answer. Very rough estimates of the populations of Chicago and Tulsa, Oklahoma (and their surrounding regions), for example, make it easy to say which is more likely to sustain a full complement of professional sports teams.

SUGGESTED READINGS

Prehistoric Settlement Patterns in the Virú Valley, Perú by Gordon R. Willey (Bureau of American Ethnology Bulletin No. 155, Smithsonian Institution, Washington, DC, 1953). The report on the fieldwork carried out in the summer of 1946 that is regarded by most historians of archaeology as the foundational work in regional settlement study. The idea that study of regional patterns of settlement distribution can inform us about ancient social organization is clearly present, although the work fails to recognize except very superficially the quintessentially demographic nature of studying "how man disposed himself over the landscape."

The Basin of Mexico: Ecological Processes in the Evolution of a Civilization by William T. Sanders, Jeffrey R. Parsons, and Robert S. Santley (Academic Press, New York, 1979). A synthetic account of pathbreaking work that established the field methods from which current best practices in regional archaeological survey are most directly descended. Includes sustained attention to regional-scale demographic reconstruction in archaeology, calling on regional archaeological survey, site-scale intensive surface survey, extensive site-scale excavation, bioarchaeological analysis of burial popu- lations, and modern and historic census data. This weaving together of multiple lines of evidence to form a basis for reconstructing regional demography has been pursued, developed, and further advanced through subsequent decades.

Settlement Pattern Studies in the Americas: Fifty Years Since Virú edited by Brian R. Billman and Gary M. Feinman (Smithsonian Institution Press, Washington, DC, 1999; distributed by Eliot Werner Publications, Clinton Corners, NY). A sampler of regional settlement archaeology in North, Mid- dle, and South America, conceived as a tribute to Willey and his Virú Val- ley work.

Archaeologies of Landscape: Contemporary Perspectives edited by Wendy Ash- more and A. Bernard Knapp (Blackwell, Malden, MA, 1999). A collection of papers arguing in various (and sometimes contradictory) ways that the notion of "landscape" broadens, enriches, or renders obsolete earlier ap- proaches to regional settlement studies. Mental processes are prominent in these chapters; demography is not.

"Regional Settlement Pattern Studies" by Stephen A. Kowalewski (*Journal of Archaeological Research* 16:225–285, 2008). Reviews still more recent re- search from around the world that takes as its conceptual foundation the distribution of people and their social groups in a landscape. Expresses a very skeptical attitude toward the mentalist variants of the landscape con- cept.

CHAPTER 2

WHAT CAN WE USE AS POPULATION PROXIES?

Contemporary census takers go around and count people (as well as asking a smaller sample of them what they do for a living, how much money they earn, where they come from, what they eat, what their religious beliefs and ethnicity are, etc., etc.). Archaeologists, obviously, can't do this directly because "our" people are long dead. We can often count people in burial contexts—and burial analysis in archaeology has come up with some inventive ways of asking these dead people what they did for a living, how much money they earned, where they came from, what they ate, what their religious beliefs and ethnicity were, and so on. Household archaeology also helps provide answers to questions like these through the study of the structural remains of residences, and especially through the careful analysis of the artifacts and ecofacts recovered from the garbage left by different households. Analysis of cemetery populations is a source of information about the age structure of the living population and helps us identify periods of local population growth and decline.

Both household archaeology and analysis of cemetery populations, however, must be based on samples selected from the ancient regional population (that is, the sites we chose to excavate or surface collect at high intensity). Because of the time-consuming nature of the data collection required for cemetery or household analysis, as well as incomplete preservation of cemeteries and houses, we cannot simply extend such approaches comprehensively across an entire region. Cemetery and household approaches, then, tell us the kinds of things census takers regularly learn from samples of larger populations. Census takers use samples for answering questions like these because it's very time consuming and costly to get this information for entire populations, and because they can be found out with sufficient accuracy by studying samples.

Such sampling approaches, however, can only be successful if census takers have already collected basic information about the overall size, structure, and spatial distribution of the entire population. Similarly, in archaeology the full interpretive potential of cemetery and household analyses cannot be realized without comprehensive knowledge about the overall size, structure, and spatial distribution of populations across a regional-scale landscape. These broader characteristics of entire regional populations are the central subject of this book. The myriad approaches to mortuary archaeology, household archaeology, and regional settlement demography are vital complements to each other in giving us different parts of the information about ancient populations that economists, sociologists, and political scientists (not to mention demographers) depend upon censuses to tell them about contemporary populations.

The initial challenge for regional settlement demography is to identify things we can observe and quantify in the regional-scale archaeological record that show a consistent relationship to overall population. Such things are often referred to as population proxies because we let them stand in for the population counts we cannot make directly. Population proxies amount to relative population estimates, since we take more of a population proxy in one place or period than in another to indicate a larger population in that place or period. Population proxies are often assumed to be directly proportional to actual populations. If we take twice as much of a population proxy in one place as in another to indicate twice as large a population in that place, we are making such an assumption of direct proportionality.

"Twice as much" is a stronger and more specific demographic reconstruction than just "more," but both are relative statements in that nothing has been said about the actual number of people. "More" could mean 5,000 as opposed to 5, or it could mean 10 as opposed to 5. "Twice as much" could mean 5,000 as opposed to 2,500 or 10 as opposed to 5, but it rules out 5,000 as opposed to 5. In this chapter and the next, we are concerned only with population proxies as *relative* indicators of regional-scale populations. In Chapter 4 we will come to actual numbers of people in the form of absolute population estimates. Quite a number of population proxies have been used at small scales in archaeology (single sites or parts of sites). We will not attempt to discuss them all here, although a few of them do merit attention in this context because it has been possible to scale them up for use as regional population proxies.

COUNTING RADIOCARBON DATES

We have chosen to emphasize the population proxies most relevant for sedentary Neolithic and post-Neolithic societies because that is the context with which we have most experience, and because there is simply not room in this small book to devote very much attention to the rather different approaches that may be required for earlier times and highly mobile populations. Before going any further, however, we must mention at least briefly one of the most frequently used approaches to relative demography for highly mobile and/or very early populations.

For sedentary populations with substantial settlements, most approaches to regional demography involve a census-like approach based on the notion that—with appropriate field and analytical methods—we can identify and quantify archaeological remains that represent a substantial majority of the human occupation that existed. For highly mobile populations, however, such as Australian hunter-gatherers, remains of occupation events may be very ephemeral and (especially at time depth like that of the Paleolithic) any instance in which enough is preserved for us to recognize and study archaeologically may be the rare exception to the rule. In such settings the accumulated radiocarbon dates in the archaeological literature for a region could be used as a population proxy. The idea is that the more people there were in a defined region at a particular time, the more remains they will have left on the landscape, the more archaeological deposits will have been discovered and excavated, and the more radiocarbon samples will have been recovered and dated. The quantity of radiocarbon dates, then, has been used as a population proxy and graphed through time to produce a curve of change in total population size. Since radiocarbon dates come in the form of probability statements (with error ranges), such a graph takes the form of a summed probability distribution. Another layer of statistical complexity is added, of course, with calibration of dates (and the unevenness of calibration curves can create its own confounding effects for using the summed probability distribution as a population proxy).

The principal concerns that adhere to this approach involve both sampling bias and the nature of the population available to be sampled from. Given that the approach is most often applied where occupation remains are scarce and the time depth great, those remains may well become increasingly scarce just from the impact of time. The more time that goes by, the more remains will be destroyed—meaning that the population of archaeological remains to be sampled from can under-represent early periods. The increasing destruction of occupation remains with time may itself produce an increasing abundance of more recent radiocarbon dates and thus a misleading impression of increasing population through time.

Archaeologists may also introduce bias into the sampling process because they may be especially interested in certain periods, leading them to preferentially select sites of those periods for excavation and artificially increase the abundance of radiocarbon dates for those periods. Another sort of bias is introduced by the common practice of seeking dates to bracket the span of an occupation. Extremely large samples of radiocarbon dates (well up in the hundreds) are needed to use them reliably as a population proxy, so it is likely that the area for which dates are summed will need to be very large—large enough to raise questions about its appropriateness for addressing the issues this book concentrates on.

Despite these challenges, summed probability distributions of radiocarbon dates are a popular population proxy for very large areas during the Paleolithic and into at least the early Neolithic—as well as for highly mobile hunter-gatherer populations where archaeological excavation has been intensive enough to yield large numbers of radiocarbon dates. These are especially challenging contexts for demographic analysis because of the extreme sparseness of remains, but for more recent periods and more sedentary populations, better population proxies are available.

COUNTING HOUSES

Among the simplest and most obvious population proxies are counts of dwelling structures. House structures are well preserved and can be counted on the surface, for example, in the dry conditions of the central Andean highlands and the nearby Pacific coastal desert; house mounds can be counted in the heavily vegetated lowland Maya area; individual rooms can be counted at many sites in the Puebloan U.S. Southwest. Most archaeologists have long been willing to assume that a site with a larger number of houses represents a larger population than a site with a smaller number of houses, and thus the Huaychamarca site in Figure 2.1 would commonly be taken to represent a larger population than the Pucusmarca site. Indeed, the Huaychamarca site—with around 80 small circular houses visible in the plan—would probably be taken by most to represent a population about three times as large as the Pucusmarca site with its 25 or so houses.

Because this is such a simple and straightforward example, it is worth elaborating on the assumptions these demographic conclusions rely on. These relative statements are, of course, comparisons between the two sites, so the assumptions have to do with comparability of data from the sites. Similarity of preservation and recording of remains are obviously important and require little further discussion. Some more interesting assumptions to explore include that:

- These small circular structures had a similar residential function at both sites.
- The houses were occupied by similar numbers of people, on average, at both sites.
- The degree of contemporaneity of use of structures is similar at both sites.
- The degree of permanence or seasonality of occupation of houses is similar at both sites.

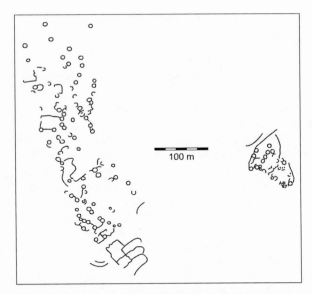

Figure 2.1. Surface remains of architecture at Huaychamarca (left) and Pucusmarca (right) in the Upper Mantaro–Tarma region in highland Peru. (Data from Parsons, Hastings, and Matos 2000:242, 246.)

Since the nature of construction and setting of the two sites is highly similar, they were both utilized during the same time period, and they are separated by only slightly more than 1 km, these assumptions seem pretty safe—so safe that even stopping to make them explicit may seem a waste of time.

We do so to make two points, though. First, the relative demographic statements we have made about the two local communities these archaeological sites represent do *not* require us to make any determination at all about just how many people actually lived in each house, or about what proportion of the houses at either site were in use contemporaneously, or about whether the occupation of any of the houses was permanent or temporary. These issues do matter for absolute population estimates (see Chapter 4), but for the relative demographic statements made above, we have only had to assume that—whatever the answers to these questions may be—they are similar at the two sites.

The second point is that the kinds of relative demographic statements we make often involve comparisons between settlements that existed in different time periods, and this may complicate the issue of comparability. Average family size might change through time, for example, and this could change the relationship between house counts and population, undermining the accuracy of house counts as a population proxy—not only for making estimates of absolute population size, but also even for relative statements across periods. Changes in seasonal patterns of occupation from one period to another could have a similar effect.

Such things do not always change through the time spans we study, but the possibility that they could must not be completely ignored (and may well, in and of itself, be an observation of importance to us). Even for such a simple and straightforward population proxy as house counts, caution is warranted. Other kinds of evidence can be sought to assess whether and to what extent such things may have changed from one period to the next. Such evidence might include change through time in average house structure size or change through time in the age structure of a population, as indicated in cemetery data. Either of these could provide ways of monitoring average family size. If average family size increases by 15% for some period, then house counts for that period might be increased by 15% to provide a population proxy comparable with the previous period. Seasonally sensitive ecofacts recoverable in household excavations can provide evidence of change in seasonal occupation patterns. If average occupation span increases from four months in one period to six months in the next, then house counts for that next period might be increased by 50% to provide a population proxy that behaves consistently through time.

In practice we may not have all the information needed to accomplish such adjustments. In this case we must use whatever relevant information is available to make a judgment about just how much uncertainty or imprecision we think this introduces into our results. Perhaps information about subsistence activities is so consistent from one period to the next that we have little concern about changes in patterns of seasonal occupation. Or perhaps something approaching fully sedentary residence is indicated throughout a sequence. These circumstances would lead to the conclusion that the consistency through time of our population proxy is little affected by changes in seasonality of occupation.

Another way to say this is that all population proxies—even the very simplest and most obvious like house counts—produce comparative statements incorporating an "other things being equal" assumption. It is always appropriate to think about just what other things must be equal for these comparisons to be valid, and to assess the risk that some of those things really might be unequal enough to require efforts at compensation. This is an idea we will return to.

COUNTING SITES

Counting houses is not usually feasible on a regional scale. Remains of Hongshan period (4500–3000 BC) house structures in northeastern China, for example, are sometimes visible on the surface in the form of ashy circles, but it is clear that the vast majority of them do not put in an appearance in this way. Indeed, it is clear that large numbers of them have been destroyed by plowing and only exist now as artifact concentrations at or near the surface. This is an example we will revisit later, but it means that Hongshan houses cannot be systematically and comprehensively counted across a regional landscape.

Even where surface traces of individual house structures are remarkably well preserved and abundant, the question of completeness of counts arises. In Peru survey archaeologists have extrapolated to sites with poor architectural preservation on the basis of areas and average numbers of houses per hectare within sites where preservation is good. In the Maya area, survey archaeologists have worried about how many house structures were so insubstantial that they do not leave any trace in the form of a house mound, and are thus uncounted in regional surveys based on counting house mounds. In most of the world, individual houses are seldom if ever preserved or visible on the surface so as to make it practical to simply count them systematically across a region.

Archaeologists most everywhere, however, have long been in the habit of observing sites and putting their locations on regional-scale maps. A count of sites, then, is a common population proxy and the one used in the brief treatment of population in the Virú Valley report. The two satellite images in Figure 2.2 make it easy to envision what future archaeologists might produce in the way of a detailed map of sites in two regions. The remains of structures, features, and artifacts from the settlements visible in the two images could yield archaeological maps like those in Figure 2.3, and we could count up the sites in each region. We might likely count 3 in the southern Oaxaca map and 12 in the northern Cambridgeshire map—although we could also count 6 and 16, respectively.

Often archaeologists implicitly assume that a site is equivalent to an ancient human settlement, so the question "Should we call this place one site or two?" is a classic discussion among the members of archaeological survey crews in the field. In a surprising number of regions in different parts of the world, archaeological survey crews have adopted 100 m as a rule of thumb for separating sites. If the separation between two artifact scatters is less than this, they are combined into a single site. By this criterion the Oaxaca map has 3 sites and the Cambridgeshire map has 13. Counting sites, though, is clearly not as simple as it might at first seem.

Some of the settlements in the Cambridgeshire tract are so small that they can escape notice at the scale of the satellite images printed here, but they would be identified in most archaeological surveys. A close look at either satellite image also reveals a few isolated residences whose remains would very likely not be recorded in many surveys, so we have not included them on the maps. They are such a tiny part of the regional demographic picture that omitting them has virtually no impact on the

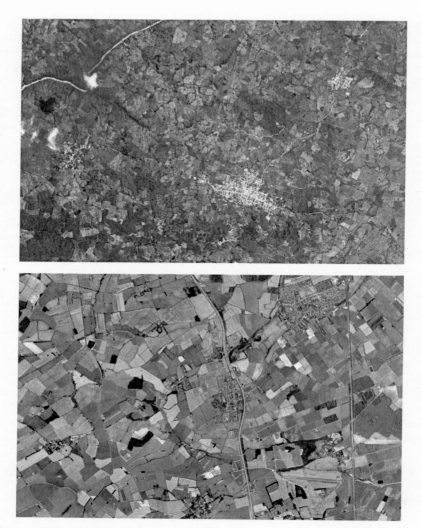

Figure 2.2. Satellite images including villages in southern Oaxaca (above) and northern Cambridgeshire (below). The images are at the same scale; they measure 11.5 x 7.5 km and thus include about 86 km². (Image sources: Google, Digital Globe, Getmapping pic.)

conclusions we might draw, although this is not necessarily the case for all regions and time periods (another point to which we will return).

Counting the recognizable archaeological sites, though, does enable us to begin a demographic comparison of the two regions. Based on this count of sites, we might conclude that this patch of Cambridgeshire has more in-

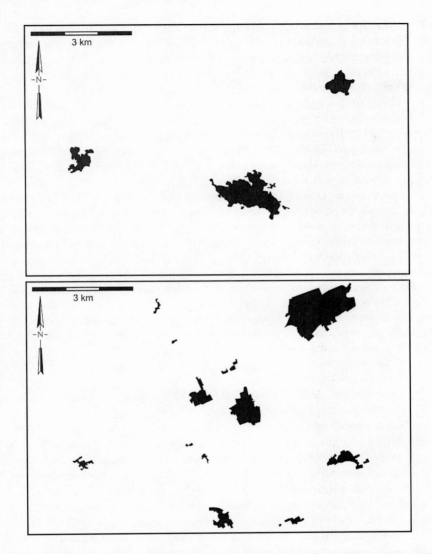

Figure 2.3. Maps of the archaeological sites that the settlements in Figure 2.2 might become by, say, the year 3000.

habitants than this patch of Oaxaca and, since the two small regions cover the same area (about 86 km²), that the Cambridgeshire map reflects a higher regional population density. These conclusions would in fact be quite correct. Census data reveal that the 12 settlements in the Cambridgeshire tract contain a total of 12,205 inhabitants compared with 5,867 in the 3 settlements in Oaxaca. If we tried to stretch our relative demographic interpretations any further, though, and say that the regional population density for the Cambridgeshire tract is four times that of the Oaxaca tract, we would be going distressingly astray. Despite the fact that it has four times as many settlements, the Cambridgeshire tract has only slightly more than twice as many inhabitants as the Oaxaca tract.

There are, of course, many cultural, environmental, economic, and other differences between Oaxaca and Cambridgeshire that affect the relationship between number of settlements and population. From this perspective it is surprising that counting sites worked as well as it did thus far. When we count sites to compare populations, it is more likely that the comparison is between two periods in the same region or between two different parts of the same region in the same period. Even in this culturally more homogeneous context, however, counting sites makes a very crude population proxy at best. If we divide the Cambridgeshire tract in half, there are 6.5 settlements in the western half and 5.5 settlements in the eastern (one falls right on the dividing line). Population is much more unevenly divided, however, with only 1,299 inhabitants in the western half and 10,906 in the eastern—where fewer but visibly larger settlements are located. This is not an unusually bad example. Number of sites just does not usually work well at all for the fundamental task of regional settlement demography: assessing in relative terms how many people lived in which locations or parts of a region.

MEASURING AREA OF SITES

This last observation about settlement size makes explicit what we ordinarily take for granted—that settlements covering larger areas usually have larger populations. And for most of the world and most of human history we see a substantial range of variation in settlement size within single regions. More than any other single factor, this variation is what makes counting sites such a poor population proxy. This has led to the very common practice of using site area as a population proxy instead.

Abandoning for the moment comparisons between Oaxaca and Cambridgeshire, let's expand the scale of our examination of settlement in each region. Figure 2.4 presents a map of modern settlements in the district of Jamiltepec, which includes 184,266 inhabitants within the boundaries of an administrative district covering some 4,200 km^2 in southern Oaxaca. The principal commercial center of the Jamiltepec district is Pinotepa Nacional, visibly the largest settlement, roughly in the center of the district; but the political capital of the district is Santiago Jamiltepec, the relatively large settlement with no very close neighbors about 25 km east-southeast of Pinotepa.

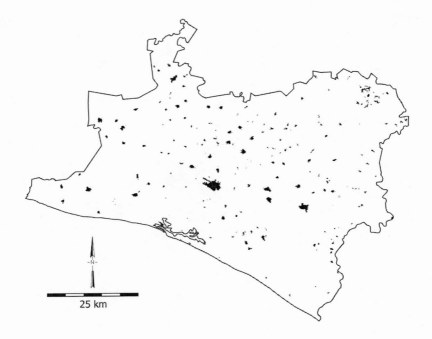

25 km

Figure 2.4. Map of the archaeological sites that the contemporary settlements in the Jamiltepec district of southern Oaxaca might become in the future. The southern boundary of the area is the Pacific coast.

Figure 2.5 expands our other example to about 1,200 km² in northern Cambridgeshire (including Peterborough) along with bits of Lincolnshire, Northamptonshire, and Rutland County. This area thus does not really correspond to anything in the political administrative system, but encompasses a roughly circular region some 40 km in diameter around the substantial commercial city of Peterborough. The region is smaller than the Jamiltepec region but it contains a larger population, numbering 270,845. Overall regional population densities, then, differ considerably between the two examples: about 230 persons/km² for Peterborough and about 45 persons/km² for Jamiltepec. (Note that the maps are not printed here at the same scale.) The data source for these maps—as for Figure 2.3—is contemporary satellite imagery, but they approximate the maps that future archaeologists might make of sites occupied early in the third millennium AD. These are maps that we can continue to compare with census data.

For the Peterborough region, some settlements contain multiple census tracts whose populations can be summed, and occasionally the areas of a few small settlements within a single census tract must be combined, but

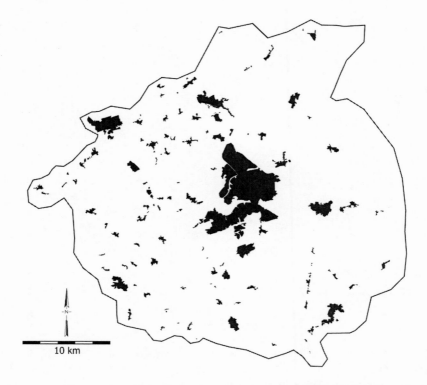

10 km

Figure 2.5. Map of the archaeological sites that the contemporary settlements in the region surrounding Peterborough might become in the future.

detailed relations between census data and settlement area can be established. The correlation between settlement area and population is extremely strong ($r = 0.996$, $p < 0.0005$, $n = 80$). As the scatterplot at the left in Figure 2.6 makes clear, though, the city of Peterborough itself is an extreme outlier whose impact could create a very misleading correlation. When Peterborough is omitted, however, the correlation remains extremely strong and significant ($r = 0.956$, $p < 0.0005$, $n = 79$). Settlement area accounts for 92% of the variation in settlement population for this region. Another way of saying this is that the residential density (number of inhabitants per hectare) within settlements in the Peterborough region is pretty constant. For future archaeologists studying the Peterborough region in the early third millennium AD, then, settlement area would serve as quite an accurate population proxy.

For the Jamiltepec region, census data are available for municipalities, which usually contain several settlements, so there is more combining of settlement areas for analysis. The correlation between settlement area and population is again extremely strong ($r = 0.974$, $p < 0.0005$, $n = 24$). As the

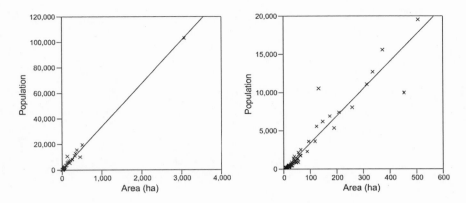

Figure 2.6. Scatterplots of settlement area and census population for the Peterborough region, including (left) and excluding (right) the city of Peterborough.

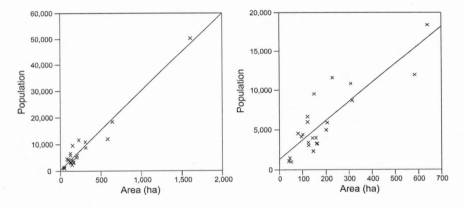

Figure 2.7. Scatterplots of settlement area and census population for the Jamiltepec region, including (left) and excluding (right) the city of Pinotepa Nacional.

scatterplot at the left in Figure 2.7 shows, the Jamiltepec region also contains one large settlement (Pinotepa Nacional) that is an extreme outlier and must be omitted for a more meaningful correlation. Without this outlier the correlation drops more than the Peterborough one did ($r = 0.866$, $p < 0.0005$, $n = 23$). Settlement area, then, accounts for about 75% of the variation in settlement population in the Jamiltepec region, and would serve as a rough population proxy—less precise than for the Peterborough region, but still serviceable.

For the area around Chifeng in eastern Inner Mongolia, China (Figure 2.8), census data are also available for townships composed of multiple settlements, and still more combining of separate settlement areas is

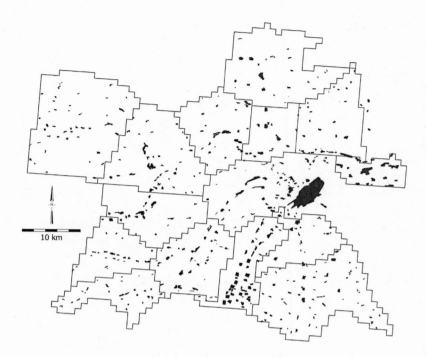

Figure 2.8. Map of the archaeological sites that the contemporary settlements near Chifeng might become in the future, based on satellite imagery like the maps in Figures 2.4 and 2.5. Administrative districts for which census population is available are indicated. The highly urbanized area of modern Chifeng city in the central part of the map is omitted from the area analyzed. (Data from Chifeng 2011a:57–59, 2011b.)

necessary to study their relationship to counted population. For this dataset the correlation is less strong than for either Peterborough or Jamiltepec ($r = 0.794$, $p = 0.001$, $n = 14$). The scatterplot at left in Figure 2.9 again shows a high outlier, which—while not as extreme as those seen in the previous two analyses—does have a very large impact on the analysis. Without this outlier the relationship between settlement area and population, although significant, is quite weak ($r = 0.351$, $p = 0.040$, $n = 13$). For these 13 townships, settlement area accounts for only about 12% of the variation in settlement population and would not serve at all well as a population proxy.

Examination of modern settlement systems as if they were archaeological data, then, yields ambiguous results concerning site area as a population proxy. The varied outcomes in the above analyses parallel similar investigations carried out with contemporary data from Mesoamerica,

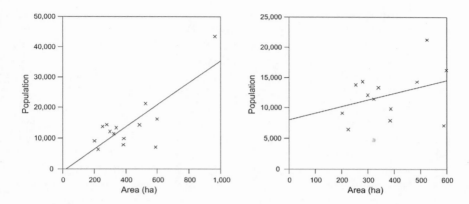

Figure 2.9. Scatterplots of settlement area and censused population for the Chifeng region, including (left) and excluding (right) the high outlier. (Data from Chifeng 2011a:57–59, 2011b.)

Peru, China, and other parts of the world. Sometimes settlement area within a region correlates well with actual populations, sometimes not; sometimes the correlation is strong but nonlinear; sometimes there are several different strong correlations for different kinds of settlements.

MEASURING DENSITY OF OCCUPATION

Fortunately, it is often possible to improve upon settlement area to create a better population proxy by assessing the varying densities at which residents are packed into settlements.

Residential Density

When the correlation between settlement area and population is poor, it means that the residential density (number of inhabitants per hectare within occupied zones) varies substantially from one settlement to another. (Residential density is not the same thing as regional population density, which divides the total population not just by the occupied areas of settlement but by the total area of an entire region—including open farmland, forests, swamps, and other unoccupied territory.) In some regions, then, there are in modern times some settlements with much higher internal residential densities than others, and for these regions settlement area is a poor population proxy. This can also happen in prehistory, making it important in at least some instances to improve upon site area as a population proxy by taking such variation into account.

The simplest source of variation in residential density is that houses may be located close together or far apart. The top and middle satellite images in Figure 2.10 show higher (about 125 persons/ha) and lower (about 35 persons/ha) residential densities resulting from different spacing of houses within settlements. If the spacing between houses continues to increase, it eventually produces a pattern of dispersed farmsteads like that in the bottom image in Figure 2.10. The houses in this satellite image are those of families that live on the land they own and farm, and the same dispersed distribution continues in all directions. Average spacing between farmsteads varies from one part of the landscape to another without forming an agglomeration that would be identifiable as a distinct settlement. A demographic distribution like this would leave an archaeological record in which nothing that could meaningfully be called a "site" in the conventional sense would exist (at least nothing that would be meaningfully equivalent to a definable human settlement). This represents the bottom of the residential density scale: houses so widely scattered that it becomes impossible to talk about residential density because there are no recognizable settlements as entities that can be bounded and treated as units.

To say the same thing more abstractly, settlements are visible in satellite images as spatial clusters of houses separated by unoccupied space. In similar fashion we customarily define archaeological sites as spatial clusters of archaeological remains separated by space without archaeological remains. This is the basis of the conventional (if usually implicit) assumption that a single archaeological site represents a single human settlement. The scheme works just fine for many regions and periods, but not for all. Some demographic distributions, like the one at the bottom in Figure 2.10, simply do not show spatial clustering. If there is no reasonably well-defined clustering in a demographic distribution, then it cannot be dealt with in terms of settlements and its archaeological remains cannot be dealt with in terms of sites—because sites and settlements, as such, do not exist. There is more to say on this subject later, but for now let's return to the simpler and more conventional context in which archaeological remains form the well-defined spatial clusters on the landscape that we are accustomed to identifying as sites, each of which we take to represent a well-defined human settlement.

Intensity of Occupation and Surface Artifact Density

When we can define and delimit the spatial clusters of archaeological remains that we call sites, we can measure their areas, and if the residential density in the settlements those sites represent is more or less constant, the areas can serve as a population proxy. If residential density varies substantially from settlement to settlement, though, we will need to try to improve upon area as a population proxy. The fundamental observation most

Figure 2.10. Closely spaced houses, creating high residential density within a settlement in Oaxaca (top); houses spaced farther apart, creating a lower residential density within a different settlement in Oaxaca (middle); and dispersed farmsteads not organized into separate settlements at all in Huila, Colombia (bottom). All three images are at the same scale; each is 500 m x 300 m. (Image sources: Google Earth, Digital Globe.)

often exploited in this effort is that, other things being equal, more people produce more garbage. If a settlement covering an area of 1 ha contains 50 people, garbage in and around the settlement will accumulate twice as fast as it would if that same settlement contains 25 people. Unless we are dealing with the archaeology of periods recent enough to have efficient transportation technologies, garbage is not usually moved very far from its point of origin.

In regional settlement demography, archaeologists have often turned to observations of the density of archaeological remains to give some sites more demographic weight than others. The most abundant and best preserved remains of human garbage for many places and periods are ceramics and/or lithics, and this abundance can be considerable. For example, ethnographic observation of the Tunebo at Cobaría, living a technologically rather simple life in Colombia, yields an estimate of over 6 kg of broken pottery per person per year. The community of some 500 people, then, will have produced over 700 metric tons of sherds where they have been living for something over two centuries. This averages out to almost 60 kg of sherds per ha across the entire area of their settlements.

Artifacts will accumulate in larger quantities per hectare if the number of people per hectare within a settlement is greater (once again, other things being equal). Put in its simplest form as an archaeological observation, few would argue with this principle. Imagine arriving at a hitherto unrecorded site with a colleague; it covers about 1 ha and is only detectable by close inspection because, despite good surface visibility, artifacts are extremely sparse. We would not be surprised if our colleague remarked, "Not much occupation here." The next day, at another site of the same size but with artifacts so dense on the surface that several are crushed underfoot at each step, the same colleague might well say, "Really impressive occupation here." Our colleague might balk at labeling these remarks demographic interpretations based on surface artifact density, but that is what they are. If they don't mean that more people spent more time making more garbage at the second site, then they mean nothing interesting at all.

The idea, then, that high surface artifact densities at residential sites indicate greater accumulations of garbage from more intensive and/or longer-term occupation is not novel. We can put a finer point on the idea by making explicit that "more intensive and/or longer-term" here implies something that we might measure in units like person-years of occupation. High densities might be created by large numbers of people living close together for some time, or smaller numbers of people living less closely packed together for a longer period of time, or some other combination of these variables.

We are, however, also accustomed to the idea that longer-term and more intensive occupations of a place lead to deeper stratigraphic accumulations. If this is so, shouldn't the continual production of debris bury earlier remains in whatever amounts they exist? Why should surface densities increase as occupation continues over a longer time? Part of the answer is in natural processes, like freezing and thawing, that bring buried artifacts to the surface. The most important factor, though, is probably that people dig holes. They make storage pits, wells, ovens, house foundations, cuts to level sloping areas, borrow pits to get dirt for embankments or platforms, and other kinds of excavations. Dogs, rodents, and other creatures that are often present in human settlements add to the digging. If people have only lived in the place for a very short time, what comes out of those holes is mostly just dirt. But if people have lived in the place for a long time, what comes out of those holes and gets spread around the surface includes artifacts from earlier occupations that combine with and add to those currently being dropped and discarded. The longer people have lived in the place (and the deeper the stratigraphic accumulation), the larger the quantity of earlier artifacts brought up from these excavations of varying depths and added to the current accumulation from discard. There is, then, some reason to think that both deeper stratigraphic accumulations and higher surface densities of artifacts can indicate more person-years of occupation.

Surface Artifact Density and Other Indicators of Intensity of Occupation

All of this is just idle speculation about the plausibility of taphonomic processes, though, without some actual empirical evidence that at least sometimes it actually does work out this way. Initial observations in the Basin of Mexico settlement study ran along these lines. Sanders and his colleagues took for granted that more sites meant more people and that bigger sites meant more people. They also shared the archaeological common sense that sites with very high densities of surface artifacts meant more people and sites with very low densities of surface artifacts meant fewer people.

Then they began to observe numerous Aztec-period sites (the latest sites in the pre-Hispanic sequence they studied) where surface remains of residential architecture were well preserved and they could count houses. Some of these sites were very sparsely occupied, with only 1 or 2 houses/ha; others had as many as 20 houses/ha. They found that the sites with very few houses per hectare consistently corresponded to very sparse surface artifact scatters, while the sites with many houses per hectare had much denser surface artifact distributions. While in the field they observed the same phenomenon in the contemporary villages they walked through. The ground was littered with much more broken glass, plastic, and ceramics in villages with many houses packed closely together, but such debris was less dense in villages with houses spaced farther apart. Other archaeologists have made the same observation about contemporary villages in the regions where they work.

Systematic comparison of surface artifact densities and information from stratigraphic excavation for sites 342 and 674 in the Chifeng region provides a different kind of empirical example of correspondence. Both sites had occupations from several different periods extending back more than 6,000 years, so the relevant surface artifact densities are those of sherds pertaining to different periods, taken separately (an issue considered more fully below). Systematic surface collections were made at multiple locations spread across the sites prior to excavating small stratigraphic tests, also scattered around the sites. At a very small scale, the correlation between surface sherd densities for each period and the stratigraphic deposits that lay beneath was not good. That is, the quantities of sherds and the depths of stratigraphic accumulation for each period in a test pit were not well predicted by the densities of ceramics pertaining to different periods in a single systematic surface collection at or adjacent to the location where the test was excavated. Especially in a complex multicomponent site, such observations can vary quite erratically over distances of only a few meters.

More broadly speaking, however, there was very good agreement between the conclusions reached separately from surface and stratigraphic information about the overall extent, intensity, and distribution of occupation for each period. At Site 342, for example, systematic surface collections were made at 88 locations spread across roughly 5 ha of occupation and 10 small stratigraphic tests were dug. In Warring States times (600 BC–200 AD), occupation was sparse and patchy. Surface densities of Warring States ceramics indicated somewhat different positions for the patches than stratigraphic testing did, but both revealed a sparse and patchy occupation of roughly the same total area (Figure 2.11). Surface densities showed both some sparse occupation and some gaps in occupation in places where no stratigraphic test was located. Stratigraphic tests were not located in these parts of the site because they would have interfered with growing crops, and this is the sort of thing that happens more often in the real world of digging scattered test pits than in making surface collections.

For the next earlier period, Upper Xiajiadian (1200–600 BC), both surface ceramic densities and stratigraphic accumulations suggested roughly 4 ha of fairly continuous occupation—including about 0.6 ha of higher-density occupation—although the two sources of information located these zones in somewhat different positions (Figure 2.11). For still earlier Lower Xiajiadian times (2000–1200 BC), an even larger area of fairly sparse occupation and two smaller patches of higher-density occupation were indicated by both surface densities and stratigraphic accumulations, and this time both sources of information placed these zones quite similarly (Figure 2.11).

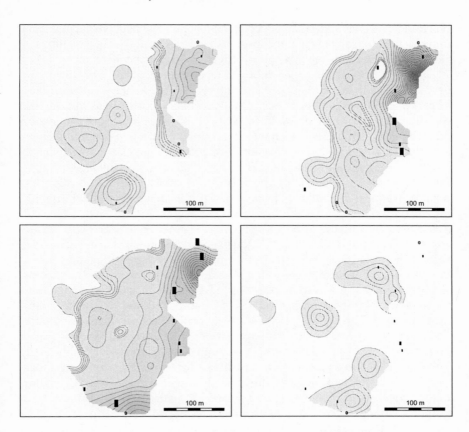

Figure 2.11. Occupation at Site 342 in the Chifeng region as indicated by surface densities of sherds of different periods: Warring States (upper left), Upper Xiajiadian (upper right), Lower Xiajiadian (lower left), and Hongshan (lower right). Darker gray indicates higher surface densities. Larger black rectangles are stratigraphic tests with larger amounts of ceramics; smaller black rectangles are tests with modest amounts of ceramics; 0's are tests with no ceramics. (Data from Chifeng 2011a:69–72, 2011b.)

The earliest period represented at Site 342 was Hongshan (4500–3000 BC). As for Warring States times, both surface densities and stratigraphic tests indicated a sparse and patchy occupation of roughly similar size. That the locations of the patches do not match very precisely is not surprising, given that the Hongshan period began 6,500 years ago; that there is a total of perhaps 2,200 years of occupation at the site following the Hongshan period; and that even in the stratigraphic tests no Hongshan material was found in situ—all was redeposited. In sum, the conclusions we would reach about area and density of occupation at Site 342 from surface ceramic densities and stratigraphic accumulations agree quite well, despite considerable overall time depth and multiple periods of occupation.

In the Upper Daling region of western Liaoning Province, China, investigation of 16 ha of Hongshan period residential area revealed remains of pits and other Hongshan occupational features preserved in situ, and with very little in the way of surface or subsurface remains of other periods. The entirety of these 16 ha were examined by surface collecting crews moving back and forth across them 5 m apart and sticking small survey flags into the ground next to all surface sherds. This made the areas of highest surface densities in each part of the 16 ha easily visible (although just what the highest density was in each part of the area varied substantially). In 24 separate sectors, grids of 5 x 5 m squares were intensively surface collected by screening the uppermost part of the plow zone for careful artifact recovery. This was followed by extensive magnetometer survey, covering almost 13 of the 16 ha. Finally, 27 stratigraphic tests, each 1 x 2 m, were excavated in and around nine of the 24 sectors where intensive surface collections were made. For these nine sectors, then, there is information about the intensity of utilization in the form of rigorously quantified surface densities of Hongshan sherds, magnetometry, and stratigraphic excavation.

The results of the magnetometer survey were especially interesting in two areas. In one the magnetometry extended from a sector with high surface sherd densities some 150 m out into a larger zone, where the initial flagging of artifacts indicated substantially lower surface sherd densities. The magnetometer imagery corresponded very closely to this pattern, with a much higher density of magnetic anomalies of probable cultural origin in the area of higher surface sherd densities, declining to a much lower density of such anomalies where surface sherd density was lower (Figure 2.12).

In another sector, in the interval of a few months between intensive surface collection and magnetometer survey, the entire surface was modified to create an orchard. The top 20 cm or so of soil were dug away and piled in earthen embankments or berms, forming a grid of squares about 3 m on a side with a fruit tree planted in the lowered center of each. Magnetometer survey still revealed signatures of cultural features, but more relevant to the present discussion is that the earthen berms separating the planting squares showed up as strong positive anomalies. This is probably a consequence of cultural activity—such as burning and decomposition of organics—which converted weakly magnetic minerals in the soils to more strongly magnetic forms, making a sharp contrast between the raised berms and the exposed subsoil within the squares. These positive anomalies were strongest (and thus the outlines of the squares darkest) in precisely the part of this sector where surface sherd densities were highest. Thus these two indicators of the intensity of ancient use of the locality corresponded very well.

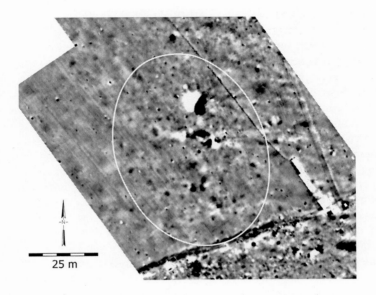

Figure 2.12. Magnetometer survey from the Upper Daling region. Ellipse indicates area of higher surface artifact densities. Magnetic anomalies of probable cultural origin show as dark areas against lighter gray background. That these anomalies are less abundant outside the area of higher artifact density is seen most clearly to the north and west and at the southeast corner. Bedrock interference along the eastern and southern edges makes the contrast more difficult to see. (Data from Peterson et al. 2014a, 2014b.)

In the nine sectors of this same study for which stratigraphic data are available to compare with surface artifact densities measured by intensive surface collection, there is once again very good correspondence between the two indicators. For each of these nine sectors, surface sherd densities are the average of at least ten 5 x 5 m collection squares (and as many as 50) and the number of sherds produced per test pit is the average for as many as five stratigraphic tests, excavated to sterile soil (for only one sector is there just a single test). The correlation between the surface density of Hongshan sherds and the number of Hongshan sherds per stratigraphic test is strong and significant ($r = 0.892$, $p = 0.001$, $n = 9$). Once again, then, surface sherd density works well as an indicator of intensity of occupation in a place, as judged by an independent source of archaeological information.

COMBINING DENSITY WITH AREA

These examples do not prove that surface artifact densities will always give a reliable indication of intensity of occupation, but they do demonstrate that this can be the case in a variety of regions. Where we do have reason to believe that this is the case, we can make use of this knowledge as a way to improve upon site area, if area does not seem a sufficiently precise population proxy for the region we are working in.

The approach to using this knowledge devised in the Basin of Mexico settlement study was by way of a typology of archaeological sites. The typology was constructed according to estimates of residential density in several categories of absolute numbers. A light surface sherd density for a particular period meant a sherd on the ground every 20–30 cm without areas of higher density, and was taken to represent a residential density of 5–10 persons per ha; a moderate surface sherd density meant 100–200 sherds/m² and was taken to represent 25–50 persons per ha; and so on. Light-to-moderate occupation was intermediate between light and moderate. At the top of the scale, heavy surface sherd densities were continuous at 200–400 per m² and represented 50–100 persons per ha. For each site the total areas of surface sherd scatters at each density level were converted to numbers of inhabitants, which were then summed to give a population estimate for the settlement. For example, a site with 2 ha of light Early Classic surface sherd density and 1 ha of moderate Early Classic sherd density would mean 2 ha of occupation by 5–10 persons per ha and 1 ha of occupation by 25–50 persons per ha, for a total estimated population of 35–70 inhabitants.

The approach taken in the Basin of Mexico, then, does rely on both area and density as the basis of demographic analysis, but it moves very directly from separate observations of area and density to estimates of absolute numbers of people, without any stage in the calculations that is exactly a population proxy. We will remain in the world of relative estimates (or population proxies) in this chapter and the next, and defer closer examination of the basis for estimating absolute numbers until Chapter 4.

The other principal way of combining observation of variable densities of surface artifacts with site areas uses a continuous scale of measurement rather than breaking down artifact density and residential density into categories. For each defined patch of occupation for which a density has been measured for surface sherds of a particular period, the area of the patch (usually measured in hectares) is multiplied by the surface sherd density within it (usually measured in sherds/m²). The product is an area-density index that depends on both variables. A higher value for the area-density index is produced by either a larger area for the surface scatter, or a higher density of sherds within the surface scatter, or both. A higher value for the area-density index thus corresponds to more intensive utilization of the place during the period the sherds pertain to. A surface sherd scatter covering 2 ha with a surface density of 5 sherds/m^2, for example, yields an area-density index of 10. A surface sherd scatter half as big (1 ha) with a sherd density twice as high (10 sherds/m^2) yields the same area-density value of 10.

It is accurate to think of the area-density index as a way to quantify the garbage on the landscape. If surface sherd densities do provide a reasonably good indication of the densities of ceramics in the accumulated stratigraphic deposits of their period in a location, then the area-density index is an indicator of the total amount of sherds of that period in that place. It does not provide an indicator of the absolute number of sherds there, but only a relative indicator. A higher area-density index means that there are more sherds in that place either because they are spread across a larger area, or because they are packed more densely, or both.

Under most circumstances sherds are produced primarily by breaking ceramics in ordinary, daily residential activities and they are disposed of as garbage, often becoming the primary component of that garbage that is well preserved for centuries in a wide variety of environmental conditions. The area-density index is thus a relative indicator of the amounts of garbage produced in different places during the period to which the sherds counted pertain. If *on average* in a particular cultural context, the amount of garbage (or, specifically, sherds) produced per person per year is relatively constant, then the area-density index is a relative indicator of something like the person-years of garbage deposited in a place during the period to which the sherds pertain. More person-years of garbage deposited in a place mean more person-years of occupation in that place—which is to say, on average through time, a larger population.

Table 2.1 illustrates how an area-density index works out for a simple, fictitious regional archaeological dataset. The region contains five small sites where sherds of Period 1 were regularly found at relatively low surface densities. The sites vary somewhat both in terms of area and surface sherd density and these values are multiplied together for each site to produce an area-density index in the table. The area-density index is finished off by dividing it by the number of centuries in the 300-year-long period so that it will be easier to compare with other periods that may be longer or shorter. Since the largest site also has the highest surface sherd density, the final area-density index suggests a greater range of variation in settlement populations than either area or density does on its own.

As time goes on in this example, some substantial demographic changes are evident. By Period 2 the number of settlements has nearly doubled and there has been spatial expansion at previously existing settlements. The surface densities are also higher, in particular at four settlements that truly stand out for much higher densities than the others. The areas and densities are combined into an area-density index, which is then divided by the

Table 2.1. Calculation of Area-Density Index for the Settlements in a Hypothetical Region for Each of Four Periods

	Period 1 (300 years)				Period 2 (300 years)				Period 3 (300 years)				Period 4 (600 years)			
	Area (ha)	Density (per m²)	Index	Index ÷ Centuries	Area (ha)	Density (per m²)	Index	Index ÷ Centuries	Area (ha)	Density (per m²)	Index	Index ÷ Centuries	Area (ha)	Density (per m²)	Index	Index ÷ Centuries
	1.0	2.8	2.80	0.93	1.7	4.3	7.31	2.44	0.8	3.9	3.12	1.04	0.9	3.3	2.97	0.50
	0.8	2.1	1.68	0.56	0.9	15.9	14.31	4.77	1.3	4.0	5.20	1.73	1.1	4.2	4.62	0.77
	0.9	3.8	3.42	1.14	1.5	3.7	5.55	1.85	1.2	2.8	3.36	1.12	0.7	4.5	3.15	0.53
	1.2	3.6	4.32	1.44	1.3	22.3	28.99	9.66	1.1	4.1	4.51	1.50	1.4	3.8	5.32	0.89
Sites	1.7	4.2	7.14	2.38	6.3	4.3	27.09	9.03	0.7	2.7	1.89	0.63	0.9	8.9	8.01	1.34
					4.3	5.3	22.79	7.60	1.0	3.3	3.30	1.10	1.3	11.0	14.30	2.38
					4.7	19.7	92.59	30.86	4.3	14.3	61.49	20.50	1.0	9.5	9.50	1.58
					5.1	17.6	89.76	29.92	6.7	17.8	119.26	39.75	1.6	10.7	17.12	2.85
					6.8	4.7	31.96	10.65	4.9	21.4	104.86	34.95	0.7	7.4	5.18	0.86
													1.3	8.5	11.05	1.84
													6.8	26.1	177.48	29.58
													5.9	36.4	214.76	35.79
													4.7	33.4	156.98	26.16
Total			19.36	6.45			320.35	106.78			306.99	102.33			630.44	105.07

number of centuries in the period (again three). The final population proxy values divide the settlements into three clear groups: three with values less than 5, four others with substantially higher values between 7 and 11, and two that combine both large size and high density for a much higher population proxy value around 30. The sum of the population proxy values for individual settlements is slightly over 100, well above the value for Period 1, suggesting regional population growth by a factor of over 15.

The total regional population proxy remains about the same in Period 3 but the population distribution across settlements has changed quite dramatically. There is now a sharp differentiation between six relatively small, low-density settlements and three much larger ones with substantially higher densities of surface materials. A very large proportion (some 93%) of the region's population would appear to be crowded into these three very large, dense settlements, while a very small minority lived in a few sharply different small, less densely packed communities.

A similar total regional population and distribution across communities persists in Period 4, with three very large, dense communities and a number of much smaller, less dense ones. The number of small communities has increased slightly and the proportion of the regional population in the three large communities has decreased a bit (to about 87%). Both densities and areas are substantially higher on average than in Period 3, but dividing the product of area and density by the number of centuries in the period has the effect of attributing these increases mostly to the fact that the period is twice as long as the previous ones.

An area-density index is thus a continuous-scale population proxy based on the dual notion that more people in a place for a longer time will usually mean either garbage (i.e., sherds) spread across a larger area, or garbage (i.e., sherds) accumulated at greater density within an area, or both.

CHRONOLOGY AND CONTEMPORANEITY

As already implied, chronology is usually dealt with in regional settlement demography in the same way it is dealt with in most aspects of archaeology: in terms of a sequence of periods. The things archaeologists have tried counting as population proxies are usually first sorted out according to the periods they pertain to, and then counted. Radiocarbon dates are an exception; they are inherently chronologically specific, so counting radiocarbon dates produces an appealing summed probability curve through continuous time that does not need to be subdivided into discrete periods.

When houses are counted for a site or a region, houses of each period are counted separately. Especially when the period is much longer than the useful life of a house of the kind being counted, serious worries arise about contemporaneity. If 10 families (and their descendants) live in a place for

200 years, each family in a house that on average lasts 50 years before it must be replaced, then that place should accumulate the remains of 40 houses. This may well make that place look like a village of 40 families to an archaeologist.

Contemporaneity is thus a serious issue in counting houses. Sometimes remains of earlier houses will be destroyed in the process of building new ones, sometimes not. If there are large numbers of non-contemporaneous houses at a site, the number of ones whose plans overlap may increase and thus signal that counting houses would overestimate the momentary population. Only occasionally do the specifics of the deposits at a site make entirely clear in some idiosyncratic way just how much of a discount should be applied to compensate for counting houses that were not actually occupied contemporaneously.

It is even more unusual to be able to make powerful assessments of contemporaneity in those instances where houses can be counted across an entire region. The usual hope is to achieve greater chronological precision by reducing the lengths of the periods to which the houses can be assigned by their associated artifacts to something not much longer than the useful life of a house. This level of chronological precision has been achieved in only a few regions. For individual sites absolute dating of individual structures (most often by radiocarbon or dendrochronology) can help with this problem. In regions with a long history of extraordinarily intensive archaeological research and highly precise chronometric dating (such as portions of the U.S. Southwest), sufficient information of this kind may accumulate to be useful on a regional scale.

Dealing with chronology by periods is almost automatic in counting sites for a region, since this usually means counting sites separately for each period in a region. It must be recognized that sites can, and often do, have occupations during multiple periods. The practice of simply classifying sites as pertaining to one period or another will not do; each site must be counted for each period during which it was occupied. It cannot escape notice that multicomponent sites often have quite substantial occupations in one period and much less substantial ones during other periods. This makes simply counting sites an even worse population proxy than it seemed above, when we considered the practice in a synchronic context.

Chronology by periods is also virtually automatic in dealing with site areas and surface artifact densities. Chronologically sensitive artifact attributes are usually essential. Most often this means a ceramic typology that makes it possible to use the characteristics of a single sherd to assign it to a period. Sometimes, although less often, lithic artifacts can be used in this same way. Most frequently, characterizing surface "artifact" scatters really means surface sherd scatters, since it is sherds that are the most chronologically distinctive. Other classes of artifacts and ecofacts that can be recovered from careful stratigraphic excavations seldom play much of a role in regional settlement demography because, in contrast to sherds and lithics, these other classes of material are only rarely preserved well enough to recover consistently on the surface.

For multicomponent sites areas must obviously be measured separately for each period, which means delineating the artifact scatters of each period separately. The common practice of simply recording a single maximum area for each site will not do. If surface artifact densities are to be used in some way, then they too must be determined separately for each period. These tasks have seemed either logically impossible or impractically time consuming to many archaeologists. They are neither. They were recognized as challenging in the Basin of Mexico project and solutions were offered, put into practice, and described fully in print. Another 40 years of regional survey have yielded further refinements. Since these are largely issues of data collection in the field, they will be addressed in Chapter 5.

Even when careful observations of area and surface artifact density are made separately for each period in a sequence, contemporaneity can be a complicated issue. The uses to which we put population proxies often implicitly assume them to be something like reflections of a momentary population at some time during an archaeological period. Of course settlements, like the archaeological sites they eventually become, have life spans that do not necessarily obey the ceramic style rules that divide time into periods. The sites that show evidence of occupation during a period may include not only those that were occupied throughout the period, but also some that were founded before the period began but abandoned during the period; some that were founded after the period began and continued to be occupied after it ended; and some that were founded after the period began and abandoned before it ended. To the extent that this is the case, not only counting the sites of a period but also adding up their areas will over-represent a momentary population.

If this process has a similar impact on all the periods in a sequence, then the changing value of site area by period through time still provides a proxy population graph for the region with the same shape that a graph of census-based momentary population figures at the same intervals would have—thus approximating the timing, direction, and relative magnitude of population changes. If the impact of the timing of settlement founding and abandonment differs from period to period, however, it will affect the shape of this graph. One suggested method of coping with this problem departs from the assumption that very few sites are likely to be founded or abandoned so quickly exactly at the beginning or end of a period that they show no evidence at all of the ceramics of the immediately preceding or following period. If most of the sites occupied at the end of one period and the beginning of the next will have ceramics of both, then a proxy for the momentary population at the boundaries between periods could be based on the numbers or areas of such sites. There is the additional problem that some sites with ceramics of two periods might have been occupied only during the middle of each and not at the boundary between them, but an approach like this has sometimes been used.

Approaches based on both area and density of surface artifact scatters compensate for this process in a different way. An area-density index is, as noted above, most directly a proxy for the amount of garbage produced through time and relates to population on the assumption that—other things being equal—more people produce more garbage. Consequently, sites representing occupation through only a part of a period will accumulate less garbage than sites representing occupation by the same number of people through the entire period. An area-density index value of, say, 40 represents some number of person-years' accumulation of garbage. That could mean many people in a place for only a few years, or it could mean fewer people and more years, but all the years would be within the period the ceramics counted pertain to.

A community of 100 people living in an area of 1 ha throughout a period should leave an archaeological site with a much higher artifact density than a community of 100 people living in an area of 1 ha through only half the period. And if these latter 100 people moved to live in another 1 ha area in a different place for the other half of the period, they would leave another relatively low-density 1 ha archaeological site there. The value for an area-density index corresponding to 100 people living in 1 ha throughout the period would be quite similar to the sum of the area-density values for two sites where 100 people had lived in 1 ha, in each case through half the period.

Thus an area-density index does not differentiate between longer-term occupations by small numbers of people and shorter-term occupations by more people (all within a single distinguishable archaeological period). The same number of person-years of garbage (i.e., occupation) could be produced by either. In this way an area-density index is a proxy for aggregate occupation in a place, which can be thought of in units like person-years. This makes it important to consider the impact of archaeological periods in a single sequence, which—as is often the case—vary substantially in length. If longer-term occupation by a constant population produces larger occupied areas and/or higher artifact densities, then an area-density index will be higher for longer archaeological periods simply as a consequence of that longer temporal span—an obviously undesirable effect. It is to compensate for this effect that the area-density index for a period is usually divided by the length of the period (see above).

NONRESIDENTIAL ACTIVITIES

In some archaeological regions, it is common practice to classify sites into mutually exclusive categories—most notoriously habitation sites, cemeteries, and ceremonial sites—although a number of other special-function site categories have also come into use. Some healthy skepticism is in order in using such categories. The practice of classifying sites in this way can become reified to the point where any evidence of a grave (or public architecture) at a site causes it to be classified as a cemetery (or ceremonial site) *instead of* a habitation site and to be treated as if no one ever lived there. If this really does seem to be the case, then such a site (or its area or its sherd density) should probably not be included in a population proxy.

The problem is that burial and ceremonial activities very often take place within or immediately adjacent to habitation areas. In our experience this is demonstrably the case in some regions where standard practice rigidly classifies sites either as habitations or cemeteries, for example, but never both. If burials (or ceremonies) are actually closely associated with habitation areas, then classifying any site with visible evidence of burial (or public architecture) as a non-habitational site and excluding it from contributing to a population proxy may cause substantial deflation of population proxy values. One must insist on some real evidence that an archaeological site was not used for habitation before taking such a step. Such evidence can readily come in the composition of the surface artifact assemblage. If the surface sherds simply do not include those from kinds of vessels used in ordinary daily household activities, then the site was probably not habitational.

On the other hand, it is sometimes the case that a substantial proportion of the surface artifact assemblage at a cemetery or ceremonial site is composed of sherds from vessels of the sorts used in daily household activities. It might be argued that these sherds result from temporary occupations associated with ceremonial or funerary occasions. At least if the population proxy being used is based on area and density, though, these sherds should be included in it. They represent residential garbage being left on the landscape that is, during the time of those temporary occupations, not being left elsewhere (and thus not being counted in the population proxy). Sherds recognizably specific to burial offerings or ceremonial activities might well be excluded from these calculations wherever they occur. This is especially important if there is one period when such artifacts are especially abundant and might unduly inflate the population proxy, making it less comparable to those of other periods.

OTHER THINGS BEING EQUAL

As advertised early in this chapter, we have qualified much of what we have said with "other things being equal." Just what other things must be equal will vary from case to case, depending on the nature of the archaeological record in different regions. It is worth mentioning a few of the common ones, though, and what might be done if they are not in fact equal. The previous section is just such a discussion. The issues of sites or artifacts not connected with the garbage of daily living will likely not be a problem for a population proxy if these issues play out in very similar ways in all periods in a region. If some periods in a particular region had many more non-habitational sites, or produced substantially more artifacts not involved in daily residential activities, then it is particularly important to document this and carefully exclude such remains from the calculation of a population proxy.

Also as noted above, an area-density index based on sherds of different periods assumes that the average amount of broken pottery produced per person per year is constant from one period to the next. With sufficient smaller-scale data from more intensive work at individual sites, it may be possible to document that this is not the case. One may, for example, estimate that pottery use increased at some point and that thereafter the number of sherds produced per person per year was twice what it had been before. Knowing that at least this "other thing" was not equal throughout the sequence, and approximately how unequal it was, leads to an obvious way of coping with the problem. The population proxy calculated for periods following the increase in pottery utilization can simply be divided by two to allow for this change. It will then be comparable to the population proxies calculated for earlier periods. It is worth noting that this has very seldom actually been done in regional settlement demography. It certainly could be done in any instance in which changes in the rate of pottery utilization were documentable, however, and in which estimates of the total amount of pottery used per person per year have been made on the basis of site excavations.

The scheme for pottery classification must also provide for equal recognizability of the sherds of different periods. This is especially a worry if many sherds wind up in an "unidentified" category. If, for example, only 30% of the sherds from a regional survey are identifiable to period, then using those sherds to arrive at an area-density index assumes that about 30% of the sherds *of each period* have been identified. If only 5% of the sherds of one period have been identified, then the population proxy for that period is clearly an underestimate. If pottery classification depends mostly on things like rim form and decoration, many sherds are likely to be left unidentified, but a far higher proportion may well be identified for periods when decoration was common than for periods when decoration was not common. The best way of dealing with this issue is to devise a ceramic classification scheme that relies primarily on characteristics of paste, temper, and surface that are observable even on the small body sherds that usually make up the bulk of a surface collection. This can provide a path to a reasonably confident assignment to period for the vast majority of the sherds collected.

More discussion of other things that may not be equal will be pursued in chapters 4 and 5 in connection with absolute population estimates and with the methods for carrying out field survey so as to produce data that can sustain regional demographic analysis.

CONCLUSION

As we go on in the next chapter to review some of the kinds of analysis that are based on population proxies, we usually have either an area-density index or just site area in mind as the population proxy, since these are the two archaeological observations that stand in for population most often in systematic treatments of regional settlement demography. Under the right circumstances, site area can be a good population proxy. An area-density index will do a better job for regions where artifact densities vary substantially in different sites, and where they can be reliably and efficiently assessed in the field.

Certainly other proxies have been used, and used convincingly, in particular instances. There is no one proxy that is the best choice for all situations. Archaeologists deal with an extremely wide range of kinds of societies, demographic structures, and settlement systems. Perhaps more important, the nature of the archaeological record varies enormously from region to region. The best archaeological population proxy is the one that produces the most convincing results in the particular circumstances it has to deal with. It is always worth paying explicit attention to just how convincing the chosen population proxy is in a particular study. Sometimes it is possible to apply several different population proxies that make different assumptions; it is reassuring if they lead to similar conclusions. Regional-scale archaeological population proxies, however, must always be taken as approximations.

The kind of detailed information that comes from more intensive smaller-scale studies at individual sites provides another opportunity to assess how well a regional-scale population proxy is working, and possibly to improve it. For example, as noted above, an area-density index in its simplest form assumes that the average number of sherds from broken pottery produced per person per year remains relatively constant. If excavation or intensive surface collection makes it possible to estimate populations at a few sites from other kinds of evidence, then the validity of this assumption can be assessed and—if necessary—the direction and magnitude of changes in pottery utilization estimated, so as to provide correction factors for the area-density index.

SOME QUESTIONS AND ANSWERS

1. When an area-density index is used as a population proxy for periods of uneven lengths, it is common to divide it by the length of the period, since the combination of area and density is likely to increase simply as an effect of a longer occupation span. If area alone is used as a population proxy, is it appropriate to divide it by the length of the period for the same reason? Why or why not? How might you allow for the impact of differing period lengths on area as a population proxy?

Whereas the amount of garbage produced by a given number of people (and thus the density of archaeological materials) might be expected to increase in direct proportion to the length of the occupation, the same is not true of occupied area. For a single farmstead in a dispersed settlement pattern, some ethnoarchaeological observation has shown that the area of the garbage scatter increases with time. The increase is fast at first but soon slows down. Much the same might be expected at the scale of a village settlement as houses decay and are replaced. Some of their replacements will be constructed beyond the previous settlement limits, thus expanding the occupied area, but many will be built within existing settlement limits and thus not have the effect of increasing overall settlement size.

In general, then, it does not seem wise to divide site area as a population proxy by length of period, since this would substantially overcompensate for long periods. It is possible, for a given regional dataset, to play long periods off against each other to estimate how strongly length of period affects occupied area. For example, in the Valle de la Plata, Colombia, the total occupied area for the 1,000-year Formative period can be compared with the totals for the three subperiods that comprise it. Not surprisingly, the total occupied area for the Formative is greater than the total for any of the three subperiods. When compared with three periods of about 300 years, the total for the 1,000-year Formative appears to overcount occupied area—not by a factor of three but only by some 36%, and this figure can be used to adjust numbers for other long periods down to a standard 300-year equivalent.

2. Would the total number of sherds of each period recovered in a survey be a useful population proxy? Why or why not?

The total number of sherds of each period recovered in a survey would not be a very reliable population proxy in most circumstances, because it depends on the dubious assumption that the proportions of sherds by period in the survey collections accurately reflect the proportions of sherds by period that are out there in the landscape. The survey collections almost certainly do not represent an unbiased sample of the total population of sherds that exists in a region. For one thing, the rare sherds of early periods are likely to raise the enthusiasm of survey crews who collect every one they see, while they remain immune to this desire insofar as the abundant sherds of other periods are concerned. This creates a substantial sampling bias in favor of early sherds, making it seem that the early population was much higher than is really the case.

Such sampling biases can be combated with appropriate field methods (see Chapter 5), but even so the total number of sherds is not a very reliable population proxy. More insidious effects that are impossible to compensate for adequately are also likely to cause biases. For example, surface collections from sparse shallow sites will almost inevitably include a relatively high proportion of the sherds that exist at these sites, whereas surface collections from very dense, deep sites will include a much smaller proportion of the sherds that exist at these sites. Since sparse sites are likely to be much more common for some periods than others, the total number of sherds in the survey collections will systematically over-represent those periods.

3. When archaeologists classify sherds, we sometimes create various uncertain categories. That is, in addition to sherds of Period 1, Period 2, and Period 3, we may have sherds assignable to "Period 1 or 2," "Period 2 or 3," and "Period 1 or 2 or 3." How could you use such a classification as the basis for an area-density index, or even for assigning an occupied area to a period?

A ceramic classification that includes uncertain categories like "Period 1 or Period 2" (or "certain Period 1," "probable Period 1," and "possible Period 1") is simply not very appropriate for regional demographic analysis. Archaeologists in such a situation who just ignore the uncertain categories have sometimes wound up with collections in which more than 90% of the sherds are ignored. Basing demographic conclusions on the remaining 10% or less will not do because the impact of this uncertainty is sure to fall more heavily on some periods than on others. Sometimes the validity of an analysis can be maintained by grouping short periods together into longer ones with which most of the sherds can be identified. A more effective approach is to carry out ceramic analysis in full awareness of the fatal biases that large numbers of unidentified sherds will introduce into the data. Schemes for ceramic classification must not be based largely on form and decoration attributes visible on only a small proportion of sherds, but must rely largely on paste, temper, and surface characteristics visible on the vast majority of sherds. It will probably be necessary to risk educated guesses about the period a sherd pertains to, since if even as many as 5% or 10% of the sherds remain unidentified and are thus excluded from the analysis, the potential impact on demographic conclusions begins to be worrisome.

4. In dry regions of the Near East and South Asia, an occupation site is often a mound (a tell *or* tepe*) that rises above a flat plain. Surface artifacts may be relatively scarce since these mounds consist mostly of large volumes of collapsed and compressed mud brick architecture, which accumulates higher and higher with time. How could you adapt the area-density index idea to these circumstances?*

For sites like Near Eastern tells, the volume of the mound has sometimes been used as a population proxy, based on the assumption that such tells mostly consist of the compressed remains of collapsed mud-brick architecture. Especially if this is mostly residential architecture, then the volume of tell accumulation for a period (divided by the length of the period, if the periods are of dissimilar lengths) would be roughly proportional to the population. For tells that accumulated through multiple periods, the area covered in each period might be detectable from surface artifacts, but the depth of accumulation for each period would probably require some form of subsurface testing.

5. We have discussed the area-density index in the context of sedentary settlements. Could it be a valid population proxy for a highly mobile population? Why or why not?

The logic of an area-density index is just as valid for a mobile population as for a sedentary one, and considering how it applies to mobile residence patterns helps make clear just what that logic is. As an attempt to quantify the amount of garbage accumulated in a place, the area-density index is specifically a proxy for person-years of occupation in that place. That is why we expect to get the same area-density value for 100 people living in 1 ha for 100 years as for 50 people living in 1 ha for 200 years. That same area-density index could also indicate 100 people living in 1 ha for six months each year for 200 years or 25 people living in 1 ha for three months each year for 1,600 years. Any one of these combinations amounts to 10,000 person-years of garbage (that is, occupation).

The area-density index does not in and of itself tell us which of these possibilities is indicated, but it does provide an approximate indication of the aggregate amount of occupation. Typically the length(s) of the period(s) represented among the artifacts set a maximum time span for the occupation (and thus simultaneously a minimum number of people). The shorter the period(s), the more accurate these numbers are. Whether occupations for the given period and region are year-round or seasonal (as might be the case for mobile residence patterns) requires additional archaeological evidence that might need to come from the excavation of a sample of sites. If both year-round and seasonal occupations occur in the same region and period, the artifact assemblage would likely make it possible to determine which category a particular site belonged to, perhaps based on more knowledge from excavation of a sample of sites.

6. If house roof technology changes from thatch to ceramic tile at a particular point in a sequence, it may be the case that a large proportion of the sherds from after this change are roof tiles. Should they be counted in the density values used for an area-density index? Why or why not?

Starting to make house roofs of ceramic tiles certainly counts as a change in the rate of ceramic usage per person per year. If roof tiles were included in the ceramic counts on which densities were based, the resulting area-density index might still be a perfectly good population proxy, but it would surely not be comparable to the area-density index from a period prior to the use of ceramic roof tiles. Exclusion of roof tile sherds from the ceramic counts would seem an essential first step in maintaining comparability of the area-density index through time. If houses through the entire sequence being studied were roofed with ceramic tiles, the inclusion of roof tile sherds in the ceramic counts would not necessarily pose a problem.

7. If the rate of ceramic utilization (and thus the number of sherds produced per person per year) changed at some point in a sequence, we might want to make an adjustment to an area-density index following that point to maintain comparability with earlier periods. What kind of information might we use to determine ceramic use rates? How would we use this information to adjust the area-density index?

The logical principles for determining ceramic use rates from archaeological data, at least, are relatively straightforward. Suppose, for example, that a site covering 1 ha has been investigated with 100 randomly placed stratigraphic tests, each 1 x 1 m. This amounts to excavating 1% of the site's area (and volume), so if the tests produced a total of 5,246 sherds, then we would estimate that the site as a whole contained 524,600 sherds— and with the complete data we could put an error range with this estimate and the others below, so as to know just how precise we should take them to be. Based on the area of house floor encountered in the tests, we might estimate that the total area of house floor at the site was 536 m^2, and additional excavation data could enable us to say that on average there were 8.5 m^2 of house floor space per person. This would lead to a population estimate of 63 inhabitants for the 1 ha settlement. Radiometric dating might provide 150 years for its occupation span. Thus 9,450 person-years of garbage is represented by 524,600 sherds, for an average of 56 sherds per person per year. If similar calculations for the preceding period yielded a ceramic use rate only half as large (an average of 28 sherds per person per year), then the area-density index for that preceding period would need to be multiplied by 2 for comparison with the second period.

There are at least a few regions in the world where the abundance of published archaeological data of the right kinds would actually make it possible to do something like this. There are more where enough fieldwork has been carried out to make it possible, but detailed quantitative data have not been made publicly available. Excavation reports that simply describe what the sherds look like, without giving information about just how many of which kinds came from where, however, do not provide the necessary empirical basis for this kind of analysis.

SUGGESTED READINGS

"The Use of Summed Radiocarbon Probability Distributions in Archaeology: A Review of Methods" by Alan N. Williams (*Journal of Archaeological Science* 39:578–589, 2012). An exploration of the sample size needed for using radiocarbon dates as a population proxy, as well as of the confounding effect of calibration curves and the impact of progressive destruction of remains over time. The context in which these methodological issues are worked with is, essentially, tracking change in the total population of the Australian continent over the past 40,000–50,000 years.

"Radiocarbon Dates as Data: Quantitative Strategies for Estimating Colonization Front Speeds and Event Densities" by James Steele (*Journal of Archaeological Science* 37:2017–2030, 2010). A consideration of how accumulated radiocarbon dates can be used to map gradual movements of populations across space—in this instance, initial colonizers of the North American continent.

Demographic Archaeology by Fekri A. Hassan (Academic Press, New York, 1981). A broad treatment of many aspects and implications of demography for archaeology. Chapter 6 is especially relevant to the methodological concerns discussed in this chapter. It reviews approaches taken in different regions to quantifying living space, house structures, rates of artifact discard, and rates of food consumption (and thus ecofact content in garbage). All these things have served as population proxies at the scale of a single archaeological site, and some of them have been scaled up to serve as population proxies for larger regions.

Prehispanic Settlement Patterns in the Lower Santa Valley, Peru: A Regional Perspective on the Origins and Development of Complex North Coast Society by David J. Wilson (Smithsonian Institution Press, Washington, DC, 1988). Working in a region with excellent architectural preservation, Wilson could count houses at some sites and extrapolated their densities within sites to others where preservation was not so good (see pp. 75–80). As in the Basin of Mexico, absolute estimates of population numbers were built into the population proxy from the ground up. The Santa Valley project provides raw material for examples in future chapters as well.

Settlement Patterns in the Chifeng Region by Chifeng International Collaborative Research Project (Center for Comparative Archaeology, University of Pittsburgh, 2011). Details the use of an area-density index in the Chifeng region of northeastern China, and is the source of some of the empirical illustrations presented above of the relationship between surface artifact density and other means of assessing the density of occupation in a settlement. Examples in later chapters draw heavily on the Chifeng research.

Hongshan Regional Organization in the Upper Daling Valley by Christian E. Peterson, Lu Xueming, Robert D. Drennan, and Zhu Da (Center for Comparative Archaeology, University of Pittsburgh, 2014). The Upper Daling data and methodological explorations appear in a number of places in this and later chapters.

Prehispanic Chiefdoms in the Valle de la Plata, Vol. 5: Regional Settlement Patterns edited by Robert D. Drennan (University of Pittsburgh Memoirs in Latin American Archaeology, No. 16, 2006). For an area where vegetation interferes with assessing surface artifact densities, this report makes an argument that these densities are uniformly low and thus area provides a good population proxy. Data from the Valle de la Plata and the larger region of which it is a part—Colombia's Alto Magdalena—are used extensively in later chapters too.

"Incorporating Variation in Occupation Span into Settlement-Pattern Analysis" by Robert E. Dewar (*American Antiquity* 56:604–620, 1991). An approach to the problem that, especially for a long period, a map of occupied areas may be a palimpsest of places not occupied contemporaneously. Dewar develops a means to assess momentary regional populations at the points of transition from one period to the next.

"Ceramic Breakage Rate Simulation: Population Size and the Southeastern Chiefdom" by Timothy A. Kohler (*Newsletter of Computer Archaeology* 14:1–20, 1978). Estimating the number of sherds produced per person per year for demographic purposes.

"Empirical Bayesian Methods for Archaeological Survey Data: An Application from the Mesa Verde Region" by Scott G. Ortman, Mark D. Varien, and T. L. Gripp (*American Antiquity* 72:241–272, 2007). An innovative Bayesian statistical approach to assigning settlement evidence to short periods, for a dataset including copious detail but collected by different projects, using different field methodologies and a variety of (less precise) chronological schemes.

CHAPTER 3

WHAT CAN WE DO WITH POPULATION PROXIES?

Many of the vital demographic analyses in regional settlement research do not necessarily require determination of absolute population numbers. They can be based directly on the kinds of population proxies discussed in the previous chapter. In the hope of making clearer just how that works, we turn to a selective review of some such analyses before continuing in Chapter 4 to the issue of converting population proxies into actual numbers of inhabitants.

REGIONAL POPULATION GROWTH AND DECLINE

Regional population stability, growth, or decline are fundamental demographic observations easily based on archaeological population proxies without need to make estimates of absolute numbers. Figure 3.1 shows population change in a portion of the Chifeng region of northeastern China according to three of the population proxies discussed in Chapter 2. All three show the same broad pattern: relatively low population early in the sequence, a period of dramatic growth, followed by a substantial decline, and then more growth. Both the number of sites and the total occupied area of sites show substantial growth in the Hongshan period, while the growth shown by the area-density index is more modest.

Further examination of the data reveals that—while the number of sites increases quite substantially at this time—the period is a long one and many of the sites are quite small and have very low densities of surface artifacts. They likely represent a number of occupations that did not last through the entire period and would thus tend to over-represent the population. The area-density index, then, seems the most reliable proxy. All three agree on the extremely high rate of growth between Xiaoheyan and Lower Xiajiadian times. In Upper Xiajiadian times the number of sites decreases, but they are larger sites with dense artifacts and the area-density index reflects this well. The number of sites drops in Zhanguo-Han times

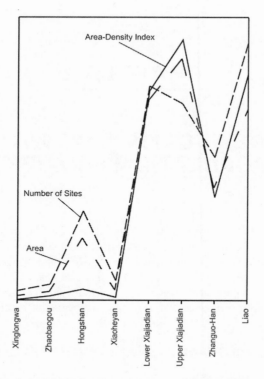

Figure 3.1. Regional demographic change through some 7,000 years as shown by three different population proxies for part of the Chifeng region. (Data from Chifeng 2011a, 2011b.)

and the sites are smaller—changes again encapsulated well in the area-density index.

Finally, sites are more numerous in Liao times and, although their areas tend to be small, the densities of surface material are fairly high for a period much shorter than some of the earlier ones. This places the area-density index between the values for the other two. The overall pattern of change in the size of the regional population is thus shown in the population proxies, and examination of where differences between the proxies come from suggests that the area-density index is consistently the best indicator.

LOCAL COMMUNITIES

Local communities are meaningful and important entities in many societies. These are the social entities to which we attach labels like "hamlet," "village," "town," and "city," although cities often press at the limits of what it seems reasonable to call "local." G. P. Murdock famously defined the local community as a social group whose members engage in face-to-face interaction on a virtually daily basis, and this definition works reasonably well for the smaller local communities (hamlets and villages). The spatial extent and population sizes of towns and cities would generally stretch beyond the limits of daily face-to-face interaction for the entire population, but they are often divided into neighborhoods that share important properties with small separate local communities.

The utility of Murdock's definition for us here is to emphasize that the members of a local community interact more frequently with each other than they do with members of other local communities. The principle that, on average, interaction decreases as distance increases is especially strong for the periods archaeologists usually deal with, which predate modern technologies of transportation and communication. This gives particular importance to the spatial clustering of residences that defines local communities, or settlements—and that also corresponds to the spatial clustering of archaeological remains into sites, which are often taken to be equivalent to human communities (as discussed briefly in Chapter 2). The distance-interaction principles behind this logic typically remain unspoken assumptions, but these are the (basically demographic) assumptions that have long been the basis of taking the site as a fundamental unit of archaeological observation and analysis. Once we recognize these assumptions explicitly, we can place our methods and interpretations on sounder footing, and sound methods for identifying socially meaningful local communities in the archaeological record are essential if we aim to study any aspect of them.

Sites and Communities

One of the fundamental elements of social change that regional demographic information enables us to monitor is change in the scale and nature of the local communities in which people live. A regional sequence of local community change might begin with a modest number of hamlets, which slowly become more numerous as some of them grow to village size at the same time, followed by the dramatic growth of one of these to a much larger-scale community we might call a town. Even a simple description like this depends on a meaningful delineation of human communities, since local communities are the units in terms of which the description is framed.

The picture changes if our archaeological data lump together what are really several separate communities or split apart a single community into several smaller ones. This can happen quite easily when sites, however they happen to be numbered by survey crews in the field, are each uncritically assumed to represent a meaningful local community. We noticed this

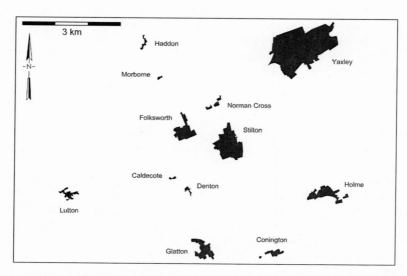

Figure 3.2. Modern settlements in a small area of northern Cambridgeshire (see Figures 2.2 and 2.3).

characteristic of contemporary settlement in Chapter 2 for a small area in northern Cambridgeshire that reappears in Figure 3.2. Here several instances of spatially discontinuous zones of occupation seem to belong together with their neighbors as single local communities. Following this intuitive sense of the most meaningful way to treat the spatial distribution of occupation in Chapter 2, we counted 12 sites. This judgment is borne out by the fact that the 16 spatially separate patches of occupation are named as 12 local communities, as shown in Figure 3.2. The commonly used rule of archaeological survey that patches of occupation separated by less than 100 m be counted as single sites comes close to this result, with 13 sites—leaving separate only the two patches that comprise Conington, which are more than 100 m apart.

At least some researchers have recognized that the arbitrary 100 m rule does not always produce a satisfactory result, especially when applied to sites without regard to the spatial shifting of occupation over time. They have moved the task of delineating sites out of the field and into the lab, making it a question of explicit analysis. Figure 3.3 shows the surface scatters of artifacts in a small area of the Valley of Oaxaca, Mexico, numbered as they might conventionally have been recorded: one very large site (No. 12 including two small surface scatters less than 100 m away to the east) and 17 smaller ones (some of these also including distinct patches of surface scatter separated by less than 100 m). The figure also shows how the

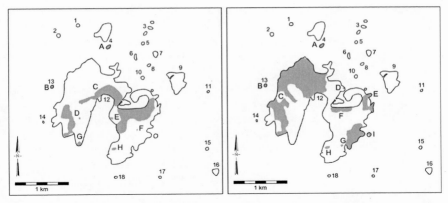

Figure 3.3. Settlement in a small area of the Valley of Oaxaca. Places with contiguous archaeological remains are outlined and labeled with conventional site numbers. Areas with Rosario phase sherds (700–500 BC) are shown in gray at left with letters indicating the analytical units that were taken to be hamlets and villages. The same is shown for Monte Albán Ia (500–200 BC) at right. (Data from Kowalewski et al. 1989.)

patches of human occupation were distributed in two of the eleven pre-Hispanic phases in the Oaxaca sequence.

The Oaxaca project defined and numbered sites separately and independently for each period, aiming to provide more meaningful units of analysis that corresponded better to the changing patterns of human communities. For the Rosario phase occupation, eight separate sites were delineated and these were treated implicitly in analysis as eight meaningful local community units. What might have been numbered Site 12, if the Valley of Oaxaca survey had followed conventional site numbering practice, became six separate units for analysis and description of Rosario phase communities. For the subsequent Monte Albán Ia phase, nine separate sites were delineated, seven of them encompassed within the boundaries of the large Site 12. Some regional surveys might have carefully recorded the total area of surface scatter for each phase within Site 12 as a quantitative attribute of this site. This would produce a dataset giving the impression that Figure 3.3 had three Rosario phase communities, two very small ones and one with 42 ha of occupation—a different picture of community structure from the five very small communities and three larger ones, ranging from 8 to 20 ha, given by the Valley of Oaxaca analysis.

Similarly for Monte Albán Ia, failing to differentiate between separate patches of occupation within Site 12 would give the impression of three minute sites and one covering 78 ha—again, very different from the five very small communities, three communities of medium size (4–10 ha), and one of 59 ha given by the Valley of Oaxaca analysis. The situation would be even worse if Site 12 were recorded as two or more sites, arbitrarily separated for convenience in the field because of the large area. This would split some occupied areas that seem meaningful to treat as local communities between two or more sites.

These different ways of delineating sites to be used as descriptive and analytical units would thus lead to strikingly different accounts of the nature of community structure. The conventional scheme of calling each place with archaeological remains a site, giving it a number, and treating it as if it were a meaningful human community throughout time, entirely fails to do justice to the information that systematic high-resolution survey coverage can provide. This has implications for how data are recorded in the field that we will explore in Chapter 5.

In the Valley of Oaxaca analysis, then, the descriptive and analytical units (referred to as "sites") were defined differently for each period, making numerous individual decisions on each possible combination of separate patches of occupation—usually following the 100 m rule. Alternatively, the delineation of meaningful local communities can be automated and approached more formally as a spatial clustering task. The spatial distribution of a population proxy can, for example, be represented as a density surface. Figure 3.4 is such a surface for the same small area in northern Cambridgeshire we have looked at before. The higher peaks in this surface represent higher population densities, in this case based on modern census data. The interpolation method for producing the surface was inverse distance weighting, using distance raised to the fourth power. Separate patches of occupation stand apart as recognizably separate peaks, but their bases spread gently outward.

This is seen most clearly in the contour map, for which very small contour intervals have been chosen at the lowest levels in order to show the slight variations in the nearly flat surface that surrounds the peaks. The heavy contour line delineates clusters by grouping the non-contiguous patches of occupation in a way that makes sense, as discussed above. These clusters correspond to the place names actually used for these communities, confirming that the spatial clustering is meaningful in this instance.

Selection of a cut-off contour is a subjective decision that takes into account the particulars of the distribution being clustered and its interpretation. Once chosen, use of the cut-off contour ensures consistent treatment of the entire distribution. The behavior of contour lines on the surface responds not only to distance but also to population, in that a peak representing a larger, denser population spreads and more easily "captures" into its cluster a small nearby place. The clustering thus reflects the impacts of both distance and population size on interaction (that is, that the intensity of interaction across a spatial separation will tend to be greater at shorter distances and/or when larger populations are involved). This kind of clus-

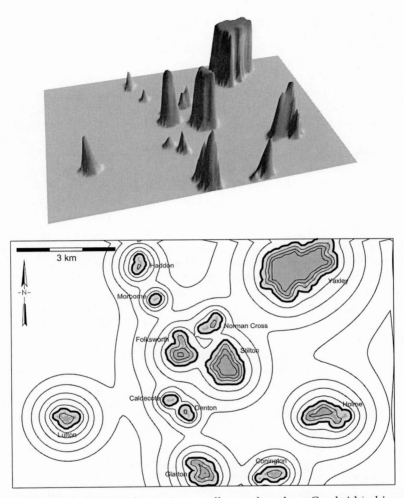

Figure 3.4. Population distribution in a small area of northern Cambridgeshire represented as a density surface (above). A map of this surface (below) provides a way to choose a cut-off contour level (heavy line) that systematically clusters noncontiguous patches of occupation (shown in gray). The contour interval in the map is not uniform.

tering simply formalizes and makes explicit the assumptions about the nature of human communities that have always underlain the archaeological urge to combine separate but nearby areas of remains into single archaeological sites. Such analysis must obviously be carried out separately for each time period after the spatial distributions of artifacts have been sorted out chronologically.

Dispersed Distributions Without Clustering

If we aim to describe or analyze the changing size and configuration of human social communities, then, we can do a better job if we do not just assume a one-for-one correspondence between such communities and archaeological sites as they happen to be defined and numbered for convenience in the field. For some regions it may make little difference, because archaeological remains occur in such tight clusters so widely separated from each other by open space that sites (as conventionally defined) reflect meaningful communities reasonably well. For other regions the spatial patterning is messier, and we can achieve better results by making the delineation of clusters an explicit analytical task—whether done purely subjectively, by a simple distance rule, or by some more formal approach. For some regions or periods, the archaeological remains may simply not show much clustering at all, and in such instances the convention of identifying sites as the basic means of recording regional distributions can produce an extremely misleading impression of ancient social organization.

Figure 3.5 shows how a contemporary dispersed distribution of farmsteads looks when represented as a density surface. In the map of this surface, no satisfactory cut-off contour can be chosen for delineating clusters of occupation that might plausibly reflect the centrally focused interaction structure of a local community. The contour level filled in by light gray shading is high enough to separate individual patches of occupation where occupation is sparse, but it leaves together as a single local community a large patch of sparse occupation running on for nearly 6 km. Raising the cut-off contour to the higher level filled in by dark gray separates this large area into parts, although each is still a very large straggling zone with minimal separation from the others. At this height the contour also entirely misses many small patches of occupation in sparser zones, providing no guidance about how they might or might not be clustered. The intermediate contour line (above the light gray level but below the dark gray) provides not a happy medium, but the worst of both worlds. This is not a failure of this approach to clustering; it is simply the way in which it shows the absence of a meaningful tendency for occupation to cluster into real local communities. Distance-interaction principles have not failed us here; interaction between these dispersed households today is very diffuse and unfocused across a large area. The apparent absence of interaction patterns strongly structured by local communities at this scale jibes with ethnographic observation.

These same differences in distributional patterning at the local scale, seen for contemporary settlement in Figures 3.4 and 3.5, are readily recognizable in archaeological data as well. At the top in Figure 3.6, clear clustering of occupation during Lower Xiajiadian times in the Chifeng region presents the unmistakable signature of well-defined local communities, as

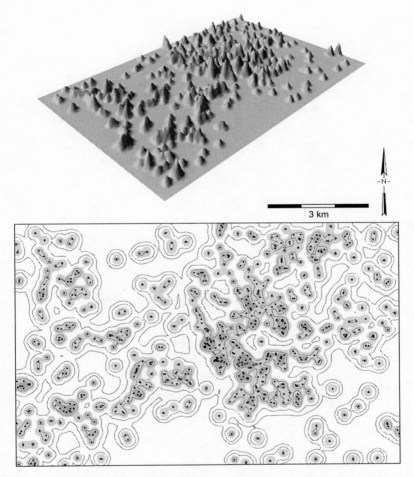

Figure 3.5. Modern population distribution in a small area of Huila, Colombia, represented as a density surface (above). A map of this surface (below) shows the impossibility of selecting a cut-off contour that satisfactorily delineates local communities because, in fact, it is a distribution without real local communities (cf. Figure 2.10 bottom).

in modern Cambridgeshire (Figure 3.2). At the bottom in Figure 3.6, the lack of clustering of the patches of occupation during Regional Classic times in the Alto Magdalena of southern Colombia is the equally unmistakable signature of very dispersed farmsteads or tiny hamlets (Figure 3.5).

A meaningful delineation of local communities in an archaeological dataset leads simply and directly to description of their sizes, locations, and distributions and how these change through time. These variables are

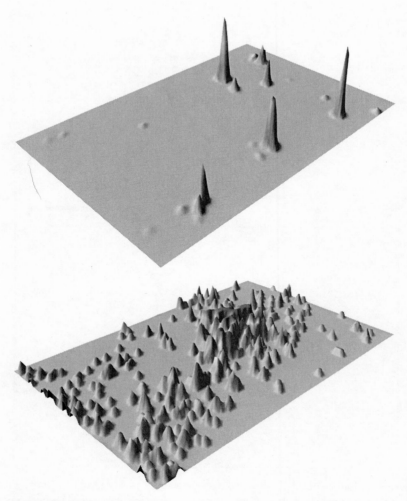

Figure 3.6. Clusters of occupation for the Chifeng region during Lower Xiajiadian times (2000–1200 BC) representing a clear local community pattern (top). Dispersed occupation for the Alto Magdalena during Regional Classic times (1–900 AD), representing little in the way of local community structure (bottom). (Data from Chifeng 2011a, 2011b; Drennan 2006a, 2006b.)

central elements in human social change, and they are of vital importance as well to considerations of how people envision their place in their social communities and in the world. Increases or decreases in average community size can be monitored, as can processes like the emergence of larger local communities. Whether larger communities emerge by internal growth or by the amalgamation of smaller communities can be determined (as can the reverse of such processes when larger communities disappear). The presence and degree of functional or status differentiation between local communities can be evaluated by comparing communities with regard to such things as architectural remains visible on the surface or proportions of artifacts with different activity or status implications. Continuity of occupation can be monitored through such simple calculations as the proportion of communities of a period that also show evidence of occupation in the succeeding period (or vice-versa), or the average distance from each community to the nearest community occupied during the previous period.

All of this must be based on descriptive and analytical units that are meaningful in social terms as local communities. Archaeological sites as conventionally defined in the field will sometimes serve this purpose, but not always. The implicit assumption that archaeological sites correspond one-for-one to real social units is irremediably embedded in all site-based description and analysis. It is not avoided by simply talking about archaeological sites rather than human communities, because the description and analysis have anthropological meaning only if sites actually *are* communities. The delineation of the units taken to be local communities should always be explicit; if it appears that archaeological sites as conventionally defined do correspond to human communities, then the reasons for believing this should be presented. Systematic use of a population proxy makes all of this possible. Estimates of absolute population numbers (Chapter 4) are not needed for delineating local communities or characterizing changes in the community patterns discussed above, although they would help us know whether a particular local community—once delineated—might plausibly be called a hamlet, village, or town.

SUPRA-LOCAL COMMUNITIES

The emergence of a larger local community that provides a central focus for various kinds of interaction at a regional scale is one of the classic hallmarks of complex social, political, and/or economic organization. The way in which regional-scale interaction may be focused on a central local community parallels the inwardly focused interaction that creates local communities. At either scale inwardly focused interaction means that individuals or households of one community interact more frequently with other members of the same community than with members of other communities.

This inward or central focus of interaction will exert centripetal forces that draw people toward each other, so as to locate closer to those with whom they interact most frequently. These are the centripetal forces that can create compact, nucleated local communities of closely spaced house-holds with high levels of interaction among themselves or, at a larger scale, regional communities focused on a central place that are separated from other regional communities by more sparsely occupied zones. Archaeolo-gists have long recognized such larger communities in the form of clusters of settlement at a regional scale, sometimes referring to them as "polities" or "districts" and sometimes labeling the more sparsely occupied inter-vening areas "buffer zones."

Clustering at a Regional Scale

In some instances these spatial clusters are clearly observable by simple in-spection of maps of settlement distributions. Mathematical assistance may make it easier to delineate them confidently and consistently. Among a number of approaches to spatial clustering, the use of density surfaces that helped us identify local community patterning above can be extended to a larger scale to provide a robust way to look at the settlement clustering as-sociated with supra-local communities. Those surfaces were produced with inverse-distance-weighted averaging, and distance can be raised to a high power to produce a surface that emphasizes local detail or to a low power to produce a more smoothed surface that reveals larger-scale patterns.

In a series of density surfaces for contemporary occupation in the area around Peterborough, local communities ranging from quite small to large in size and separated by open unoccupied space are seen most clearly in the power 4 surface (Figure 3.7), a small portion of which was examined in de-tail in the previous section (see Figure 3.4). As the power distance is raised to decreases, the inverse-distance-weighted averaging produces a smoother surface and the way a single very large local community (Peterborough it-self) dominates the demographic distribution becomes quite clear. Contin-uing to reduce the power to which distance is raised eventually produces a surface so strongly smoothed that the pattern loses clarity. For Peterbor-ough a power of 0.5 brings the picture into sharp focus, and the single supra-local community that occupies the entire region mapped (and likely extends beyond it as well) is shown in a clear, yet detailed way.

In this example we know that the demographic distribution reflects the functions of Peterborough as a central place for a supra-local commu-nity or regional-scale demographic cluster. These functions have a history that goes back to at least 655 AD when a monastery was founded there, and continued with the building of a cathedral begun in 1118, the estab-lishment of St. Peters Fair in 1189, the founding of the Diocese of Peter-borough in 1541, the growth of a major brickmaking industry after the railroad arrived in 1850, and an economy increasingly focused on com-merce and the service sector in the late 20th century.

A rather different pattern emerges when we look at contemporary demo-graphic distribution in an example from a small part of Suzhou Prefecture

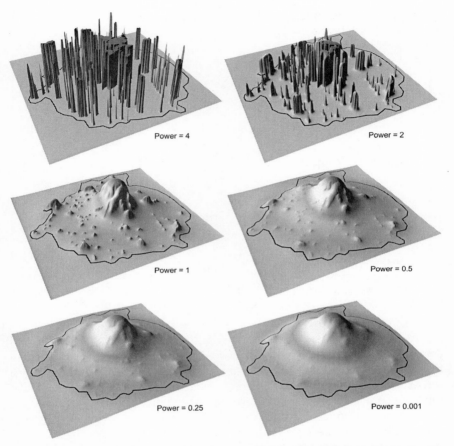

Figure 3.7. Density surfaces representing contemporary population distribution in the vicinity of Peterborough, UK, produced from the map in Figure 2.5 and modern census data. Interpolation is by inverse distance weighting with distance raised to different powers.

in Anhui Province, China (Figure 3.8). The power 4 surface in Figure 3.9 shows the compact local communities of this region. There are so many of them packed so tightly into this area that the distances between them are small, but the open spaces are so completely free of occupation that the individual local communities are easy to delineate on a power 4 surface. The regional trends are clearest in the power 0.5 or power 0.25 surface and do not show a single central demographic heavyweight—at least not within the area of this map. Instead there are about six demographic peaks of similar size separated from each other by less densely populated zones that can be used to draw the approximate limits of these entities. Such limits are shown in Figure 3.10 for the three demographic units that are more or less

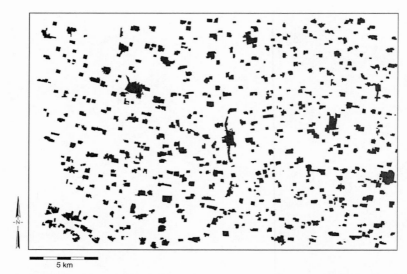

5 km

Figure 3.8. Map of the archaeological sites that contemporary settlement might become in the future for a small portion of Suzhou Prefecture, Anhui Province.

complete within the area mapped. Each of these three demographic peaks turns out to correspond to a local community that is the head of a modern township, and the limits of the demographic units provide a fairly accurate representation of the actual modern township boundaries.

These two contrasting kinds of patterns appear in archaeological contexts as well, where they have been interpreted in ways that parallel the two contemporary examples. For Monte Albán Ia times, the Valley of Oaxaca shows a pattern that resembles the Peterborough region, with a single demographic heavyweight (Figure 3.11), whereas the Chifeng region in Upper Xiajiadian times contained multiple demographic units more like those of Suzhou Prefecture (Figure 3.12). The demographic peaks around which the spatial clusters form for Upper Xiajiadian Chifeng vary somewhat more in size than those of Suzhou prefecture, but the cluster around the largest one is quite separated from the other clusters spatially and does not loom over the rest of the demographic distribution—as the single heavyweight does in the Peterborough and Monte Albán Ia distributions. This was interpreted as around a dozen separate supra-local communities, together with some additional scattered settlement that did not tend to cluster.

Archaeologists are accustomed to thinking of supra-local communities like these as composed of a central local community that might be called a "town" or even a "city" that served as a central focus of interaction, sur-

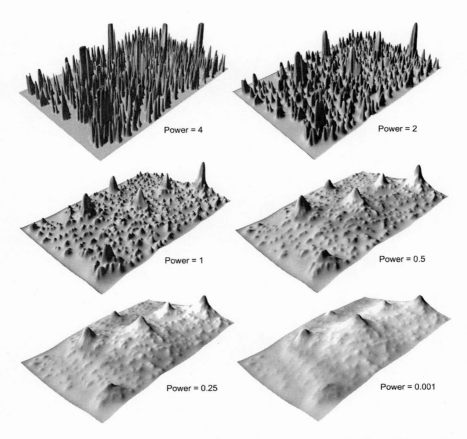

Figure 3.9. Density surfaces representing contemporary population distribution in the portion of Suzhou Prefecture shown in Figure 3.8.

rounded by a hinterland with smaller "villages" and "hamlets" that become less and less numerous out toward the margins of the supra-local community's territory. The regional-scale centripetal forces of supra-local communities, however, can also be seen quite clearly even when smaller-scale interaction is not organized into a local community structure. In such a case, small farmsteads can be packed more closely together near the central focus of regional interaction and spread farther apart out toward the margins. This is the case, for example, for the Regional Classic Alto Magdalena whose lack of local community structure was discussed above and is shown in detail in Figure 3.6. A smoothed surface of a much larger area of that same distribution (Figure 3.13) shows two separate demographic peaks of similar size, representing two separate supra-local communities

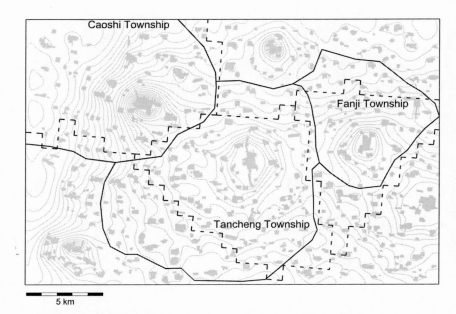

Figure 3.10. Contour map of the power 0.25 surface in Figure 3.9. Approximate limits of three regional-scale demographic units are shown as solid lines, boundaries of modern townships as dashed lines.

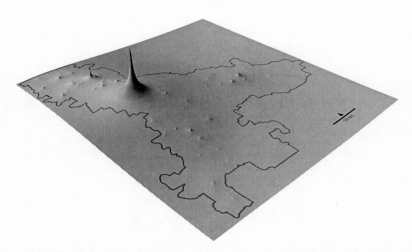

Figure 3.11. Smoothed density surface from archaeological survey data for the Valley of Oaxaca during the Monte Albán Ia phase. (Data from Kowalewski et al. 1989.)

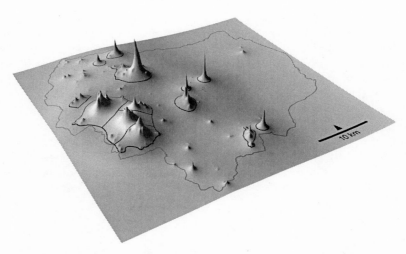

Figure 3.12. Smoothed density surface from archaeological survey data for the Chifeng region during the Upper Xiajiadian period (1200–600 BC). (Data from Chifeng 2011a, 2011b.)

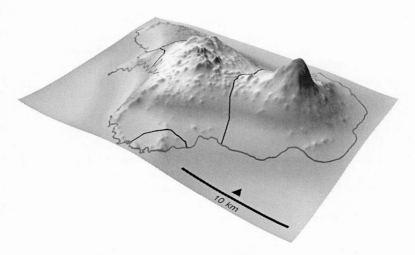

Figure 3.13. Smoothed density surface from archaeological survey data for the Alto Magdalena during the Regional Classic period. (Data from Drennan 2006a, 2006b.)

(and possibly some small fragments of others near the boundaries of the survey area). Clearly defined local communities are sometimes thought of as social building blocks of which regional-scale polities are made, but such building blocks are not essential either for the formation or archaeological identification of supra-local entities.

CENTRALIZATION AND INTEGRATION

Interaction patterns focused on a regional center play prominent roles in discussions of complex society formation, and there are tools for characterizing the strength of such centralization and the integration of supra-local communities.

Rank-Size Plots

Rank-size plots derive from the work of economic geographers who noticed for a few regions that the second largest commercial center had a population about half the size of the largest; the third largest, about one-third the size of the largest; the fourth largest, about one-fourth the size of the largest; and so on. A plot of the logarithms of these ranks (1, 2, 3, 4, etc.) against the logarithms of the local community populations produces a straight line running diagonally across a square graph, and this "log-normal" pattern thus comprises a "power law." It has never been at all clear just why one should expect this to happen, but it has occasionally been observed empirically.

Archaeologists have used such graphs to depict just how dominant a demographic position the largest settlement in a region occupies in a hierarchy of settlements, and often concluded that regions where settlement sizes follow this power law are tightly integrated under the largest settlement's domination. This situation is indicated by a rank-size plot in which the observed pattern approximates the straight-line log-normal pattern. When the largest settlement is even larger than this power law would lead one to expect, even stronger regional integration under its domination is suspected. This situation is represented by a "primate" rank-size plot in which the settlements from rank 2 downward lie below the straight-line log-normal pattern. Weak (or nonexistent) regional integration is suspected if the rank-size pattern is "convex," with the observed values lying along an arc above the straight-line log-normal pattern.

Contemporary Peterborough is a large city that overshadows the surrounding region and the very primate shape of the rank-size plot depicts just that (Figure 3.14). The Suzhou region contains several similar and separate supra-local communities, as the convex shape of the upper part of the rank-size plot shows (Figure 3.14). A rank-size plot of just one of the

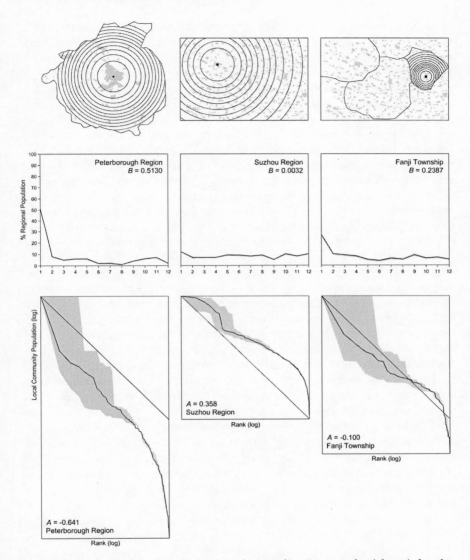

Figure 3.14. Rank-size plots (below) and centralization graphs (above) for the Peterborough region (left, see Figures 2.5 and 3.7), the Suzhou region (center, see Figures 3.8 and 3.9), and the supra-local community that corresponds roughly to Fanji Township in the Suzhou region (right, see Figure 3.10). Error zones for 90% confidence.

Suzhou supra-local communities taken by itself (the one that corresponds roughly to Fanji Township) adheres fairly closely to the log-normal line, the pattern often taken to indicate a well-integrated regional system with a dominant—but not excessively large—central local community.

Assessing the match or mismatch between observed community sizes and the log-normal pattern has usually been a question of subjective comparison of the two lines on a graph. The A coefficients in Figure 3.14 quantify the degree to which an observed rank-size pattern departs from the log-normal line. They are based on areas in a graph rectangle whose diagonally opposite corners are the ends of the log-normal line, which thus divides the rectangle diagonally into upper and lower halves. The proportion of the upper half that falls between the log-normal line and the observed rank-size line is calculated and expressed as a decimal fraction ranging from 0.0 (if the observed rank-size line is never above the log-normal line) to +1.0 (if the observed rank-size line is horizontal across the top of the graph because all local communities are the same size). The proportion of the lower half that falls between the log-normal line and the observed rank-size line is calculated and expressed as a decimal fraction ranging from 0.0 (if the observed rank-size line is never below the log-normal line) to −1.0 (if the observed rank-size line lies far below the log-normal line). This latter value can be even less than −1.0 when the graph is stretched below the lower end of the rank-size line by very small settlements at the low end of the distribution (as in the Peterborough example). A is the sum of these two values. The magnitude of the A value indicates the strength of the departure an observed pattern has from the log-normal line in either the positive or negative direction.

The issue of the statistical significance of these departures from the log-normal pattern has often been overlooked. An error range for a given confidence level can, however, be attached to the A value by bootstrapping; the same procedure can provide an error zone for representing statistical confidence graphically in the rank-size plot itself. In Figure 3.14 gray error zones for 90% confidence around the observed rank-size lines show that we can, with pretty good confidence, identify the Peterborough sample as a primate distribution that departs strongly from the log-normal line ($A = −0.641$, or between −1.064 and −0.029 at 90% confidence). Similarly, we have high statistical confidence that the Suzhou sample indicates a fairly strong convex pattern ($A = 0.358$, or between 0.285 and 0.431 at 90% confidence). The supra-local community corresponding roughly to Fanji Township in the Suzhou region—examined by itself—has only a weak departure from log-normal, and the error zone indicates very little statistical significance to this departure ($A = −0.100$, or between −0.442 and 0.341 at 90% confidence).

When used with archaeological data, rank-size plots work exactly as they do with modern census data. They can be based directly on any serv-

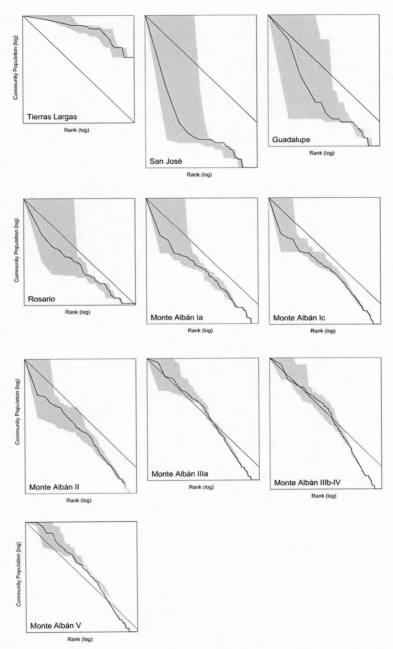

Figure 3.15. Rank-size plots for the 10 chronological phases from 1500 BC to 1500 AD in the Valley of Oaxaca. Error zones for 90% confidence. (Data from Kowalewski et al. 1989.)

iceable archaeological population proxy; absolute numbers of inhabitants are not needed. Rank-size plots can be especially helpful in tracking changes in centralization through time in a single region (Figure 3.15) and the *A* coefficient can make such tracking clearer (Figure 3.16). The high positive *A* value for the earliest sedentary settlement system in the Valley of Oaxaca during the Tierras Largas phase shows a strongly convex rank-size pattern, which shifts to a markedly primate pattern in the San José phase, focused on the burgeoning center of San José Mogote. Not surprisingly, this very strong change also has extremely high statistical significance.

The next five phases continue through the founding and development of a regional capital at Monte Albán and are also characterized by primate rank-size patterns, although not as strongly as the San José phase. We can be very confident in identifying a relaxation of the forces that produced an intensely primate pattern in San José times, but there are no changes of much significance from Guadalupe through Monte Albán Ia (since the error bars for even low confidence levels in Figure 3.16 are quite long compared

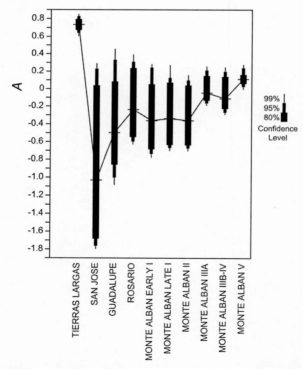

Figure 3.16. Changes in the value of the A coefficient for rank-size patterns from 1500 BC to 1500 AD in the Valley of Oaxaca.

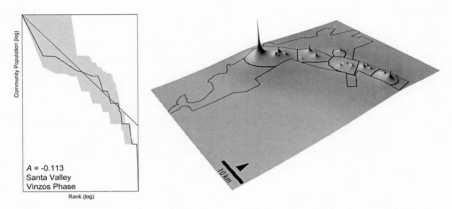

Figure 3.17. Vinzos phase (350 BC–200 AD) settlement in the Santa Valley. Rank-size plot for local communities (left), and smoothed density surface, showing supra-local community clusters (right). (Data from Wilson 1988.)

with the modest differences between *A* values for these phases). Guada-lupe occupies a transitional position between San José and the later, sig-nificantly less primate patterns.

The next major change in rank-size patterns is between Monte Albán II and IIIa, when the previous string of modestly primate patterns yields to one for Monte Albán IIIa that is not significantly different from log-normal. At the beginning of Monte Albán V, we can again confidently identify a shift, this time to a more convex pattern—interpreted as indi-cating less overall regional integration than at any time since the Tierras Largas phase, and this characterization of Monte Albán V fits well with historical documentation from around the time of the Spanish Conquest.

Rank-size plots rely strictly on the relative populations of the local communities that are their units of analysis. They do not depend in any way on the spatial distribution of these local communities and this can sometimes produce misleading results. The rank-size plot for the Vinzos phase of the Santa Valley, Peru, in Figure 3.17 shows a log-normal or pos-sibly even primate pattern (*A* = −0.113, or between −0.478 and 0.331 for 90% confidence) that would ordinarily be taken to indicate strong overall regional integration under a single center. If a large and important local community dominates a regional population, we would expect it not only to have a large population, but also to be in a relatively central position—both spatially and demographically—and to show other evidence of the special activities that draw population toward it and integrate the region.

This is true for the Valley of Oaxaca, for example; for each period in which primate or log-normal patterns are indicated, the largest commu-nity (first San José Mogote and later Monte Albán) is in a roughly central location, regional population is clearly drawn toward it, and there is architectural, artifactual, and other evidence of special activities. For the Vinzos phase, by contrast, the single largest local community—easily identifiable in the smoothed density surface in Figure 3.17—is not in a central location at all, but instead at the extreme western edge of the settlement distribution. Some nearby occupation is drawn toward it, but its centripetal forces had no visible impact on settlements more than a few kilometers away. No architectural or other evidence suggests any special function for this settlement; it seems very much like other villages, just bigger. Regional-scale clustering suggests some six separate supra-local communities of varying sizes, not the overall regional integration implied by the rank-size plot taken alone.

Rank-size plots can be useful tools but they are not a substitute for careful consideration of spatial distributions and other evidence. They can only be useful when interpreted in the context of these other kinds of evidence. Rank-size plots, moreover, cannot be used at all if settlement is not organized into meaningful social communities at the local level.

Centralization Plots

Another approach to the same basic characteristic of demographic distribution does not take meaningful local communities as the essential unit of analysis and explicitly incorporates spatial distribution as well. This approach is based on equal-area concentric rings around the demographic center of gravity of a supra-local community. The proportion of the total population in each of the rings is calculated and plotted to provide a graphical representation of how population is distributed with respect to distance from the center.

In Figure 3.14, for example, around 50% of the Peterborough region's population is located in the central ring, reflecting the primate position of Peterborough in the rank-size plot. For the Suzhou region, the demographic center of gravity (Figure 3.14) is the highest peak in the smoothed density surface represented by the contours in Figure 3.10. Again, the innermost ring has the largest proportion of the regional population, but this is only slightly more than 10%. Population is seen to be much more evenly distributed across the 12 rings, which corresponds to the convex pattern in the rank-size graph and indicates little centralization across the whole region. For just the supra-local community defined on the basis of population distribution that corresponds approximately to Fanji Township, some 25% of the population is found in the innermost ring, with decreasing proportions farther away—although this pattern of decrease is certainly not perfect. This corresponds to the roughly log-normal pattern in the rank-size graph and suggests fairly strong centralization within this township.

Converting these population proportions, ring by ring, to cumulative

Table 3.1. Example Calculation of Cumulative Percentages and *B* Value for Maximum and Minimum Centralization

Circle	Maximum Centralization		No Centralization	
	Independent Proportions	Cumulative Proportions	Independent Proportions	Cumulative Proportions
1	100%	100%	8.3%	8%
2	0%	100%	8.3%	17%
3	0%	100%	8.3%	25%
4	0%	100%	8.3%	33%
5	0%	100%	8.3%	42%
6	0%	100%	8.3%	50%
7	0%	100%	8.3%	58%
8	0%	100%	8.3%	67%
9	0%	100%	8.3%	75%
10	0%	100%	8.3%	83%
11	0%	100%	8.3%	92%
12	0%	100%	8.3%	100%
Total	100%	1200%	100%	650%
B value	(1200-650)/550=1.0000		(650-650)/550=0.0000	

proportions leads to an index to facilitate comparison of these patterns. The proportions graphed in Figure 3.14 are the independent proportions for each ring, which of course always add up to 100%. The sum of the cumulative proportions depends on how concentrated the population is in the innermost rings. Table 3.1 shows the cumulative proportions for an example of maximum centralization (100% of the population in the innermost ring) and minimum centralization (8.3% of the population in each ring). For maximum centralization, then, the cumulative proportions add up to 1200%; for minimum centralization, to 650%. This creates a scale ranging from 650 for no centralization to 1200 for maximum centralization. So that this scale will begin at 0 for no centralization, we can subtract 650 from it, and it becomes a scale ranging from 0 for no centralization to 550 for maximum centralization. If we then divide this scale by 550, it becomes much easier to use since the value for no centralization remains 0, and the value for maximum centralization becomes 1. This gives a coefficient *B* that ranges from 0.000 for no centralization to 1.000 for maximum centralization. Examination of the *B* values for the three modern examples show how this coefficient relates to the shapes of the centralization and rank-size plots and the *A* coefficient for rank-size (Figure 3.14).

Approaching centralization via the distribution of population across

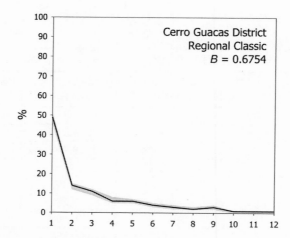

Figure 3.18. Centralization analysis for the easternmost supra-local community in Figure 3.13 for the Regional Classic period in the Alto Magdalena.

12 concentric rings makes it possible to provide a numerical index when rank-size plots cannot be produced for lack of meaningful local communities. For example, the easternmost supra-local comunity defined in Figure 3.13 for the Alto Magdalena's dispersed farmsteads yields the centralization plot in Figure 3.18. About 50% of the supra-local community's population is in the innermost ring and the proportions decline rather steadily farther and farther out. The B value of 0.675 represents even stronger demographic centralization than the modern Peterborough example.

Rank-size plots with A coefficients and centralization plots with B coefficients represent two ways to accomplish essentially the same thing: characterize the strength of demographic concentration in a defined territory. Rank-size plots approach this question via the relative populations of the local communities in a regional system, so a structure of meaningful local communities is an essential prerequisite. Rank-size plots can be soundly based on an archaeological population proxy without the necessity of deriving absolute population estimates from it, but rank-size plots make nothing of where these local communities are actually located in a region. Centralization plots with B coefficients can be used even where there are no meaningful local communities; they focus directly on the spatial distribution of a population across a region. The plots and B values require only the relative measure provided by an archaeological population proxy.

We have not, however, discussed assessing the statistical significance of differences in these B values. This can be done by providing the population proportions, ring by ring, with error ranges using standard statistical approaches to determining the error range for an estimated proportion.

For this, of course, one needs to know the size of the sample (n). It has been suggested that the estimated number of households in each ring is a meaningful sample size for that ring, based on the idea that where to live is a household decision, so the number of households is the number of independent observations the sample consists of. The error zones in the centralization graphs in this chapter are based on this approach, but this does require going beyond the relative archaeological population proxy to estimate the actual number of households the proxy represents (see Chapter 4).

Settlement Tiers

A different perspective on variation in local community population within a region has emphasized settlement hierarchy, thought of as a series of tiers—tiers that are typically equated with the levels in a hierarchy of political administration and used as a criterion for distinguishing, say, states with three-tier settlement hierarchies from chiefdoms with only two tiers. A single large central place in a highly centralized region would be identified as the top tier in this hierarchy; a second tier would be represented by a group of smaller but similar-sized settlements; yet a third tier, by a much larger group of still smaller settlements; and perhaps even a fourth tier, by a large number of very small settlements. Identification of such tiers is often sought in what are usually referred to as "site-size histograms."

It has sometimes been argued that such histograms avoid the complexities of how archaeological remains relate to population since they are usually based simply on the areas of archaeological sites. But interpreting them as settlement tiers can have no meaning except in terms of how people distribute themselves across local communities of varying population size—so site-size histograms *are* demographic analysis, implicitly but unequivocally using site area as a population proxy. Since sites are the units of analysis, they also assume a one-for-one correspondence between archaeological sites and local communities. These are not necessarily flaws, but they *are* assumptions implicit in the use of site-size histograms to identify administrative levels. Such histograms can of course be based on whatever population proxy is determined to be most accurate, and the units of analysis can be local communities not assumed to be equivalent to archaeological sites but defined through explicit analysis—both subjects we have already discussed.

The most serious obstacle to using histograms for defining distinct settlement tiers is posed by the identification of different modes. Three modes have been identified in the histogram in Figure 3.19, and these have been interpreted as reflecting a three-level administrative hierarchy and thus state-level political organization. The four settlements that make up tiers 1 and 2, as originally interpreted, however, are so spread out along the number scale that they do not really comprise second and third modes or peaks in the histogram. They are simply individual outliers from the main group of sites. If we insist on finding distinct modes, it would be more convincing to identify the two largest sites as a top tier and all the rest as a second tier, and this society would be demoted to the status of chiefdom in the article from which the example comes. The single most convincing distinction to be made between distinct modes would separate the sites at 6–9 ha from those smaller than 5 ha; then the 11 ha and 25 ha sites might become a tier, leaving the one 48 ha site as the top tier. This society would thus become a very highly developed state with a four-level administrative hierarchy. The point is that this histogram depicts a settlement population frequency distribution that, like many if not most such frequency distributions, simply does not have clearly distinguishable modes. The modes and thus tiers of settlement hierarchy defined in this histogram, then, are fictitious.

The idea that the local communities playing roles at different levels in an administrative hierarchy will fall in different size ranges does make abstract sense, but the modern world provides little empirical encouragement for thinking that these size ranges will be recognizable as distinct modes in a community-population histogram. The histogram of local community populations in the U.S. state of Idaho (Figure 3.20), for example, which would seem a relatively simple example, altogether fails to show the three modes that "should" correspond to the three-level administrative hierarchy of the state (state capital, county seats, and ordinary settlements). If we insisted on finding size modes among the larger settlements, they would not

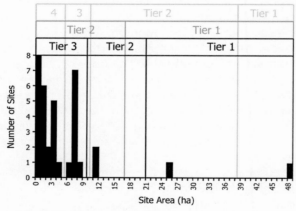

Figure 3.19. Site-size histogram for the Mengzhuang cluster of Longshan-period (2800–2000 BC) sites in Henan Province, China. Originally interpreted as a three-tier settlement system, this histogram could just as well be seen to show two or four tiers. (Data from Liu 1996.)

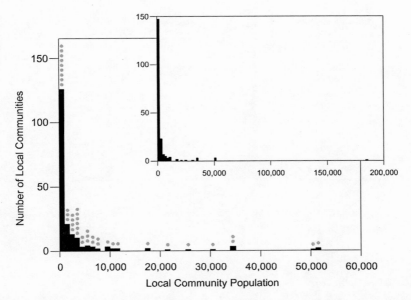

Figure 3.20. Histogram of local community populations in the U.S. state of Idaho. The state capital Boise, shown in the small histogram at upper right, is an extreme outlier. The main histogram omits Boise so as to show more detail about smaller communities. Each county seat is indicated by a dot above the bar for its size range.

correspond at all to the known hierarchy of political administration, and this is not an unusual case.

The other modern instances we have worked with reinforce the point. Peterborough stands out in a histogram (Figure 3.21) as a much larger local community than any other in its immediate vicinity, just as the rank-size and centralization plots indicate. The Suzhou region histogram (Figure 3.21) shows several high outliers, as in the rank-size and centralization plots, but they do not form any convincing peaks in the frequency distribution. The Fanji Township histogram (Figure 3.21), like the Peterborough one, shows little more than the presence of one local community much larger than all others. At a more fundamental logical level, the very idea that a well-integrated hierarchical regional system would show multimodality in settlement populations contradicts the rank-size expectation, which is explicitly a frequency distribution without such modes. In sum, conclusions about the number of levels of administrative hierarchy derived from supposed modes in site-size histograms, which have appeared frequently in the regional settlement literature, should be viewed with considerable skepticism.

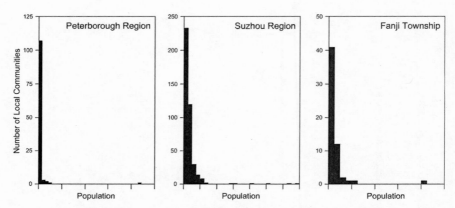

Figure 3.21. Local community population histograms for the Peterborough and Suzhou regions and for Fanji township.

Kinds of Interaction

People, on average, interact more with members of their own local communities than with members of other local communities. They interact more with members of their own supra-local communities than with members of other supra-local communities. Such communities are bounded interaction units, which is not to imply that there is no interaction across boundaries, but only to recognize that there is less interaction across boundaries at whatever scale than within them. Distance-interaction principles exert centripetal forces that pull the members of such bounded interaction communities toward each other. This force is by no means the only one acting on household decisions about where to locate, but it is among the factors involved. More frequent, intensive, and important interactions will usually exert stronger forces, pulling the interactors to locate closer to each other and tending more strongly to overcome other counteracting pulls.

These are the principles that underlie our discussion of local communities, supra-local communities, centralization, and integration, and that make it possible to recognize and delineate human social communities (and their bounds) in the archaeological record. Interaction patterns may also be more diffuse (that is, less bounded), in which case communities as social units can be not just less recognizable archaeologically; they can be genuinely less important elements of social organization. Interaction patterns can be bounded and create social communities strongly at one scale and just the opposite at a larger or smaller scale. These are all demographic elements fundamental to our accounts of human societies. Distance-interaction principles have been attenuated in various ways by the technologies of transportation and communication that have emerged during the past two centuries or so, but their impact is still strongly visible in demographic distributions on the modern landscape, and archaeologists mostly deal with much earlier periods in any event.

Although distance-interaction principles have been the basis for much of the analysis discussed in this chapter, we have thus far paid little attention to the nature of the interaction involved. It is useful to recognize and distinguish at least a few broad categories of interaction, and quite possibly some more detailed particulars as well. Archaeologists have often taken the demographic clustering and centralization they observe to be the product of interaction of a political or administrative character. Whether there is sound empirical evidence to support this interpretation is less often considered, and even the fact that other kinds of interaction can create similar patterns may not be recognized. Geographers working with such spatial patterns have tended to pay much more attention to economic interaction; ritual or religious interaction is another possibility, as is more purely social interaction. The nature of the interaction that produces some degree of demographic centralization, and thus creates settlement clusters, can have considerable theoretical importance—for example, in the study of early complex societies.

The regional patterns we have been looking at, then, do not by themselves tell us just what kind of interaction produced them. We need to ask ourselves about the context in which centralized interaction took place. That is, what activities were concentrated at a central community that drew occupation toward it? These activities that took place exclusively (or mostly) at centers, in contrast to more peripheral locations, are sometimes labeled central place functions. Their archaeological indicators include remains of special-purpose structures, features, and artifacts that occur exclusively or predominantly in demographically central locations. Sometimes this sort of evidence suggests a single sphere of activity as the main context for regionally centralized interaction and thus the strongest among the centripetal demographic forces; sometimes several different sorts of activity are involved.

For example, in the Alto Magdalena during the first few centuries AD, the most densely occupied central sectors of the regional clusters of dispersed farmsteads contained monumental funerary complexes, where important people were buried in elaborate stone-slab tombs that were covered by earthen mounds and surrounded by large-scale sculpture set up in open, level areas suitable for the assembly of substantial numbers of people. The activities for which these facilities were created are typically taken to be ritual, and these facilities appear to be the principal unusual kind of archaeological remains in demographically central locations. This pattern has been used to argue that ritual activities were an especially important context for the centralized interaction that drew the populations of the Alto

Magdalena's supra-local communities toward each other and, conse-quently, that religious belief and ritual were prime among the centralizing forces of these societies.

In the Valley of Oaxaca between about 400 BC and 450 AD, Monte Albán was the regional demographic center of gravity for a single supra-local community that occupied the entire region. Again, architecture and sculpture provide particularly strong indications of special functions for this central place. The sculptural iconography—first of the so-called *dan-zante* carvings, later of conquest slabs, and eventually depictions of rulers on thrones—speaks strongly of political and administrative activities. This is reinforced by the presence of increasingly elaborate elite residences, cul-minating in true palaces where powerful rulers lived and from which they ruled. The monumental-scale architecture includes temples as well, and the largest and most impressive buildings are arrayed around an immense main plaza that could accommodate thousands of people.

It is clear that the special activities of this central place combined reli-gious ritual with political and administrative affairs. As in the Alto Mag-dalena, however, evidence of production and distribution of goods was not especially abundant in demographically central locations, suggesting that such economic activities were not strongly developed elements in the centripetal demographic forces that created the population clusters.

At Jenné-jeno in the Middle Niger Delta between about 400 and 1600 AD, special-purpose structures, features, and artifacts suggest a rather dif-ferent sphere of activities for regionally centralized interaction in a supra-local community. Elaborate tombs, temples, monuments, palaces, and other elite residences are conspicuously absent. A substantial surrounding wall may speak to military activities and a need for defense, or possibly to reg-ulating the flow of goods into and out of the city—since concentrated pro-duction of primarily utilitarian materials like iron, ceramics, and textiles is also in evidence. Activities of an economic and possibly military nature seem to have been the context for interaction that generated regional cen-tralizing forces here.

The regional demographic patterns in all three of these examples are very similar: substantial clustering around a fairly clearly defined central point. In all cases distance-interaction principles produce the same pattern when regional-scale interaction is centrally focused. It makes no difference that interaction patterns at a smaller scale create compact, nucleated local communities in the Middle Niger Delta and the Valley of Oaxaca but not in the Alto Magdalena. The religious and ritual activities of the Alto Mag-dalena produce the same regionally clustered pattern as the ritual and overtly political and administrative activities of the Valley of Oaxaca, or the defensive concerns combined with production and distribution of util-itarian goods in the Middle Niger Delta. Regional demographic clusters, then, are the direct product of centrally focused interaction, but this cannot automatically be assumed to be any particular kind of interaction. The nature of the interaction must be determined according to evidence of the activities that are especially concentrated toward the center of the regional cluster.

Sometimes this issue is approached by way of distinguishing different site types (habitation sites, ceremonial sites, defensive sites, ceramic production sites, cemetery sites, etc.) and seeing which site type appears to be demographically central. Except for the simplest situations, though, site types are blunt instruments. As discussed in Chapter 2, they implicitly assume that each site has one and only one function, making it difficult to recognize the combinations of different functions or activities that real human communities usually contain. (The notion of "cemetery" sites is particularly overused in some parts of the world where graves may be obvious on the landscape and the mere artifact scatters that represent residential garbage often go unremarked, resulting in a failure to recognize that burials are likely to be made within or adjacent to residential areas.) And of course site types are meaningless in a pattern of dispersed farmsteads where sites cannot meaningfully be delineated. Instead of relying on site types, it is preferable to characterize the central part of a regional cluster in terms of the particular activity or combination of activities that is especially abundant there.

Functional Palimpsests

Finally, the identification of settlement clusters and supra-local communities is complicated by the possibility that the patterns created on a single landscape by different kinds of centrally focused interaction may not be coterminous. Figure 3.22 shows the results of applying some of the tools discussed above to the contemporary settlement pattern of the Jamiltepec District in Oaxaca. The smoothed surface suggests a single cluster—a supra-local community including the entire territory. Regional demographic centralization is not overwhelming, but the rank-size pattern is pretty close to the log-normal, often taken to indicate a well-integrated regional system dominated by a single central place. The histogram of local community populations reveals two outliers; it might be interpreted as indicating either a two- or three-level settlement hierarchy.

This all seems superficially to make good sense, since the territory actually consists of a modern political administrative district. The problem is that the largest settlement—Pinotepa Nacional near the center of the territory—is not the political capital of the district at all, but a large town where regionally centralized economic activities are located. The political capital is Santiago Jamiltepec, the second largest settlement, visible toward the east in the smoothed surface (Figure 3.22). The strongest forces of demographic centralization in the modern Jamiltepec district, then, are created

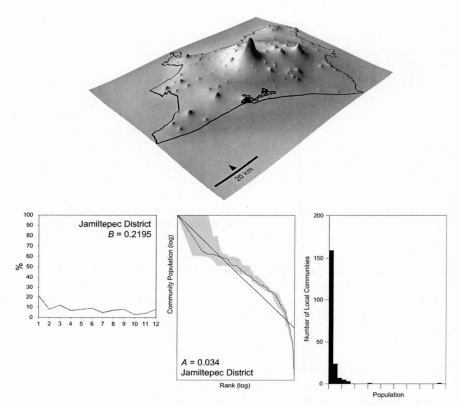

Figure 3.22. A smoothed surface, centralization graph, rank-size graph, and histogram of modern local community sizes for the Jamiltepec district in southern Oaxaca (see Figure 2.4). Error zones in the graphs are for 90% confidence.

in the context of economic interaction. Interaction of a more purely political nature also creates a demographic pull, but it is weaker and centered on a different place.

Disparate patterns of demographic centralization resulting from different activity sets can create functional palimpsests in archaeological data as well. This can be seen in the Valley of Oaxaca—which does not overlap with the modern Jamiltepec district—during Monte Albán IIIa times. The smoothed surface in Figure 3.23 suggests that we might want to divide the Valley of Oaxaca into two supra-local communities, each centered on one of the two exceptionally large local communities visible in the histogram as high outliers (Monte Albán toward the north and Jalieza toward the south). The corresponding site-size histogram was interpreted in the Valley of Oaxaca settlement analysis as a six-tiered hierarchy, with the two high outliers comprising the top tier—an observation that would ordinarily suggest two separate and co-equal supra-local communities, each with its own central place. These interpretations are also consistent with the shape of the rank-size graph, which is strongly affected by the exceptionally large size of the second largest local community (Jalieza).

The problem with such an interpretation in this instance has always been apparent to archaeologists working in the Valley of Oaxaca: in terms of the architectural and sculptural evidence mentioned above, Monte Albán and Jalieza are not equivalent at all. Monte Albán has public architecture and sculpture, both unequivocally related to ritual and political/administrative activities. Jalieza is not entirely lacking in such evidence, but its quantity and character put Jalieza in a category with at least a half-dozen other smaller settlements, from which Monte Albán stands starkly apart. There is no avoiding the conclusion that Monte Albán was the overwhelmingly dominant politico-religious center for the entire Valley of Oaxaca (and beyond).

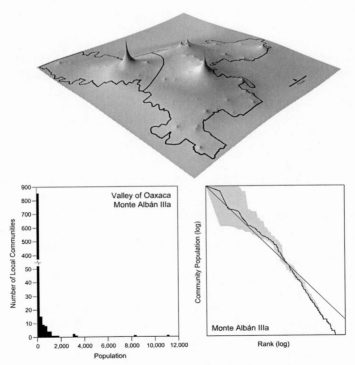

Figure 3.23. A smoothed surface, rank-size graph, and histogram of local community sizes for the Valley of Oaxaca in Monte Albán IIIa times (200–450 AD). The error zone in the rank-size graph is for 90% confidence.

Jalieza was an important place as well, perhaps with the politico-religious functions of a second-level administrative center under Monte Albán. The demographic centripetal forces it exerted, however, set it quite apart from other second-level administrative places, which had much smaller populations. The demographic patterns alone do not identify the nature of the interaction that drew such a large population together around Jalieza. It is possible that they involve the production and distribution of utilitarian goods, but the evidence of such activities is much less conspicuous archaeologically than ceremonial and elite residential architecture, and relatively little research has been done at Jalieza.

Clearly, regional settlement demography by itself does not tell us everything we might like to know about demographic clustering and settlement hierarchy. It is most useful when it can be combined with other lines of archaeological evidence—both because those other lines of evidence can add depth to our interpretations of the demographic patterning, and because knowledge of regional settlement demography provides a context in which those other lines of evidence take on more meaning. Monte Albán and Jalieza might seem to be local communities of similar population size and demographic weight in their respective supra-local communities, but architectural and sculptural evidence shows the dramatic functional difference between them and opens the door to more complete and accurate interpretation of the demographic patterns. At the same time, the regional demographic evidence makes it clear that Jalieza is different in important ways from the half-dozen second-level administrative centers to which it might otherwise be compared. This encourages us to inquire further into the nature of its role in a regional system, leading to questions we well might not ask if we had not noticed the demographic patterns.

DEMOGRAPHIC DISTRIBUTIONS AND THE LANDSCAPE

Population proxies can also serve as the direct basis for investigating relationships between demographic distributions and non-demographic characteristics of the landscape. Such characteristics of the landscape can include the more purely natural (water, firewood, wild food resources, productive soils for agriculture, pottery clay, metal ores, etc.), the more purely anthropogenic (monuments, cemeteries, etc.), and features that fall in between these two extremes (raised field systems, agricultural terraces, canal systems, defensive refuges, etc.). Our discussion of this subject will be brief because it grades into GIS analysis, which we cannot do full justice to here and which in any event is discussed in considerable detail in a number of other books. We will focus especially on some insufficiently recognized pitfalls in such analyses.

Productive soil for agriculture is the feature of the landscape we will consider; the relationship between demographic distributions and other characteristics of the landscape can be analyzed in similar ways. In particular, we will look at the relationship between agricultural productivity of soils and demographic distribution within the San José Mogote supra-local community in the Valley of Oaxaca during the Guadalupe phase. Five classes of land with varying implications for agricultural productivity (from highly productive to not productive at all) have been delineated for the Valley of Oaxaca (Figure 3.24), and the fundamental question is "To what extent does Guadalupe phase population distribution within the San José Mogote supra-local community correspond to agricultural productivity?" Archaeologists have taken a number of different approaches to answering this question, of which we will discuss only a few—beginning with one that is seductively easy, but unsatisfactory.

Data on the distribution of agricultural productivity, as well as on archaeological population distributions, are almost certain to be organized and managed with GIS software. One GIS layer might have productivity zones (as in Figure 3.24) and another, polygons representing areas of occupation during Guadalupe times. Almost any GIS program will have a tool to cross-tabulate these two layers and run a Chi-square test, and this might seem like a good way to evaluate the strength and significance of

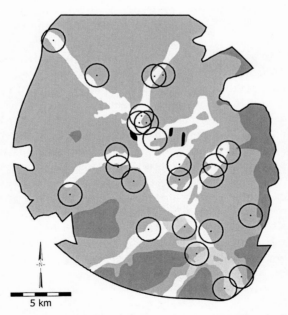

Figure 3.24. Agricultural productivity and catchment circles of 1 km radius for Guadalupe phase local communities in the San José Mogote supra-local community in the Valley of Oaxaca. Lighter colors represent more productive land.

the relationship between the two. The result for the Oaxaca data is a cross-tabulation of two rows (raster cells with Guadalupe phase occupation and raster cells without Guadalupe phase occupation) by five columns (raster cells in each of the five classes of land). The Chi-square score is 1732.077 (*df* = 4), implying a relationship of extremely high statistical significance ($p <$ 0.0005). This relationship, however, is extremely weak ($V = 0.021$), a piece of information that not all GIS programs would provide.

The serious flaw in this approach to the analysis is a product of spatial autocorrelation, a property present in almost all spatial distributions, often in much-exaggerated form in GIS raster layers that tend to have very large numbers of very small cells. The extremely high Chi-square score and significance level in this example are a consequence of the apparently very large sample size (n = 4,115,032 cells in the raster layers we used). Meaningful sample size, however, is the number of separate and independent observations, and each cell in the raster layer is not a separate and independent observation because of spatial autocorrelation.

The vast majority of cells in these two raster layers have exactly the same values as their neighbors, because even very small polygons are divided into many very small cells. This means that the value observed in each raster cell is mostly redundant with those observed in neighboring cells, so they cannot be counted as separate and independent observations. In a raster layer such as these, there is no meaningful way to say what the sample size is. Using the number of cells in the raster layer as if it were the sample size results in a disastrous overestimate of the statistical significance of the relationship, and affects the measurement of the strength of the relationship as well. This approach to studying the relationship between two spatial distributions should simply not be used.

A different approach takes the soil zones of different productive potential as the cases in the analysis. The total areas of the five soil zones in the San José Mogote supra-local community appear in Table 3.2 along with the total area of Guadalupe phase occupation in each. Even the simplest GIS software easily produces such area tabulations. In this analysis, then, area of occupation is used as a population proxy and the settlement density in the table is the occupied area in a soil zone divided by the total area of that soil zone (thus, the proportion of the soil zone that was occupied in the Guadalupe phase). The soil zones are of dramatically different total areas and we would expect some tendency for larger zones to have more population under any circumstances. The density of occupation is probably the observation that best reveals preferences for different soil zones.

Examination of the table shows some degree of correspondence between the distributions of population and agricultural productivity, at least since the two least productive soil zones have no population at all. It is not the case, however, that the most productive soil zone has either the largest or the densest population. A simple and direct way to measure the strength

Table 3.2. Guadalupe Phase Occupation in Five Soil Zones
in the San José Mogote Supra-Local Community in the Valley of Oaxaca

Soil Zone	Total Area (ha)	Settlement Area (ha)	Settlement Density
1	6,309	7.4	0.0012
2	1,059	2.9	0.0027
3	28,157	69.4	0.0025
4	5,542	0.0	0.0000
5	84	0.0	0.0000

Note: Soil Zone 1 is the most productive, soil zone 5 the least.

and significance of the correlation between population density and soil productivity is with a rank-order correlation coefficient such as Spearman's *r*. (A linear least-squares correlation would not be appropriate since soil productivity has not been measured in, say, kg of maize/ha, but only as greater and lesser.) In this instance the rank order correlation is positive (higher population densities tend to occur on more productive soils) and has moderate strength, but not as much statistical significance as we might like to see ($r_s = 0.667$, $p = 0.219$, $n = 5$). We can be almost 80% confident of this result, although those who follow the rigid null-hypothesis-rejection approach of classical statistics would surely dismiss it as "not significant" since the sacred 5% level almost universally (if arbitrarily) taken for rejecting the null hypothesis was not attained.

The reason for this outcome, of course, is the small sample size. The sample of separate and independent observations in this example is 5 (the five soil zones, each of which provides an opportunity to observe values for soil productivity and population density). The sample size can be increased if it is possible to delineate more soil zones and thus distinguish more productivity ranks, and this obviously gives a more detailed picture in any event. For the western survey zone of the Valle de la Plata, Colombia, 13 different soil zones were delineated (Table 3.3). Formative 1 period occupation shows a rank order correlation with soil productivity whose strength is similar to the correlation in the previous Oaxaca example, although the relationship is negative (higher population densities tend to occur on *less* productive soils) and the significance of the relationship is high as a consequence of the larger sample of separate and independent observations ($r_s = -0.680$, $p = 0.011$, $n = 13$).

It has often been observed that it makes sense to live not directly on the most productive agricultural soils but adjacent to them, so as to avoid reducing the amount of highly productive land available for cultivation by building structures on it. Such a pattern could be missed entirely by the analysis just discussed. A different approach is based on "site catchments,"

Table 3.3. Formative 1 Occupation in 13 Soil Zones
in the Western Survey Zone of the Valle de la Plata

Soil Zone Rank	Total Area (ha)	Settlement Area (ha)	Settlement Density (% Occupied)
13	4,451	18.6	0.4%
11.5	250	0.3	0.1%
11.5	792	6.2	0.8%
9.5	1,313	10.4	0.8%
9.5	2,807	12.8	0.5%
5.5	852	0.0	0.0%
5.5	817	16.6	2.0%
5.5	5,462	65.6	1.2%
5.5	4,118	28.5	0.7%
5.5	3,498	38.4	1.1%
5.5	2,448	20.1	0.8%
1.5	4,093	102.9	2.5%
1.5	356	5.0	1.4%

Note: Rank 13 is the most productive soil, rank 1.5 the least
(there are many tied ranks in these data). Data from Drennan
2006a, 2006b.

circles drawn around archaeological sites to delineate the resources available in their immediate environs. Values for soil productivity more precise than just ranks must be available for the different soil zones, so that the overall productivity of the catchments can be calculated based on the areas of different soils within them, but doing the calculations is an easy task for any GIS software.

The question of correspondence between population distribution and agricultural productivity is then re-framed as a correlation between catchment productivity and the archaeological population proxy. For catchment circles of 1 km radius around Guadalupe phase local communities in the San José Mogote supra-local community in the Valley of Oaxaca (Figure 3.24), the rank order correlation between catchment productivity and population proxy is negative but weak: local communities with larger populations tend to have less productive catchments. What seems superficially to contradict the first analysis of Guadalupe phase population and agricultural resources is not really a contradiction since the catchment analysis asks a subtly different question about this relationship. We have a large enough sample of site catchments (24) to give us 93% confidence in this result ($r_s = -0.379$, $p = 0.068$, $n = 24$).

Unconventional Wisdom

There are also many other analytical approaches to studying the relationship between demographic distributions and agricultural productivity (or any other characteristic of the landscape). All these approaches can be applied as well to the wide array of landscape characteristics mentioned at the beginning of this section. Mostly such analyses now fall under the GIS umbrella and there are already a good many books on GIS analysis. It is worth noting, though, that such analyses were in fact being carried out laboriously with paper maps, rulers, pencils, and graph paper or polar planimeters before the acronym GIS had even been coined. Full exploration of this subject lies beyond the aims of this book, so we will go no further, except to emphasize the four main reasons for bringing up the subject here at all.

(1) The kinds of analysis discussed in this section are demographic since they are irreducibly about how many people were where on the landscape.

(2) Different analytical approaches (like the two approaches to demographic distribution and agricultural productivity above) can ask what seem to be the same questions in subtly but importantly different ways. Some GIS software makes it easy to push buttons that perform analyses without really making clear just how those analyses formulate a general question in different ways. This puts an ill-informed analyst at risk. Some books on GIS are more help in avoiding this risk than others.

(3) This book is mostly about archaeological data, which as archaeologists we collect ourselves (see Chapter 5). The kind of analysis discussed in this brief section is likely to involve data of non-archaeological kinds as well, which as non-experts archaeologists may misinterpret or misuse. There are, for example, different approaches to categorizing the agricultural productivity of soils, some more appropriate than others for the uses we may make of them.

(4) It is increasingly easy to download data from the Internet without full appreciation of their limitations. Soil zones can again serve as an example and massive amounts of GIS data on soils are readily available for download. It may be harder to find and evaluate metadata about how the soil mapping was done, what the categories mean, how precisely their spatial limits are delineated, and how they are georeferenced. Some GIS software makes it especially easy to overlook these vital concerns. When someone says, "It must be true because I read it on the Internet," we immediately recognize it as irony—unless we're working with a GIS dataset, in which context downloading data from the Internet is often taken as a guarantee of high precision and accurate georeferencing. We overlay the archaeological data we have recorded on a soil map we have downloaded and proceed with analysis.

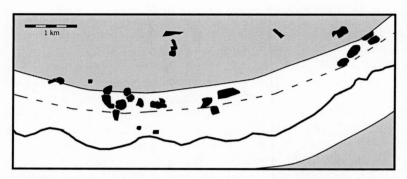

Figure 3.25. Artifact scatters overlaid on a soil map. The chain of scatters that appear to be on the valley floor alluvial soils (white) is actually located well above the valley floor on bluffs in the upland loess zone (gray). The soil map is simply not sufficiently precise to sustain meaningful spatial analysis of the archaeological remains. The boundary between the upland loess soils and the valley floor alluvial soils actually belongs at the dashed line some 300 m farther south than the boundary in the soil map. The locational discrepancy between the two maps is easily observable with the knowledge from the field that these artifact scatters are, in fact, not on the valley floor.

Unfortunately, GIS data are not immune to any of the usual Internet foibles as to source, veracity, and accuracy. Even in a source as highly respected as Google Maps, as of this writing there is a locational discrepancy of 600 m or more between map view and satellite view for much of the territory of China. As conspicuous as this discrepancy is, and whatever the reason for it, it has apparently persisted for several years. It is impossible to stress too strongly the importance of verifying that locational information from different sources is properly registered before using it as the basis of spatial analysis. This is not difficult to do since the locations of such features as rivers, highways, or valley floor margins, for example, are often detectable in different maps. Recollections of first-hand observation in the field can reveal errors in the map-overlay relationship of archaeological sites to, say, soil zones (Figure 3.25). Whatever their source, overlays of these maps should be examined carefully to see whether the same features from different maps actually do match precisely enough to sustain the planned analysis.

SOME QUESTIONS AND ANSWERS

1. What difference, if any, does it make to the interpretation of regional-scale demographic clusters if it is discovered that their more densely occupied centers correspond to areas of especially productive agricultural resources? Or if it is discovered that the more sparsely occupied zones separating them correspond to ranges of steep hills with thin soils?

If the more densely settled centers of regional demographic clusters are discovered to be on especially productive agricultural soils, or if the buffer zones between them are steep hills with thin soils, this may call into question the idea that the clusters were formed by the pulls of centrally focused interaction of some kind. Perhaps they are nothing more than the result of individual families choosing to distribute themselves across a landscape in accordance with its agricultural productivity. At the same time, a patchy environment of this sort may be responsible for creating demographic clusters that then help structure and focus human interaction of various kinds, as interaction patterns are shaped by distances in a distribution created largely by the natural environment. If the existence of regional demographic clusters can be shown to be at odds with the distribution that would be optimal with regard to resources, then we can be more confident in assigning a more powerful role in cluster formation to centripetal forces of a social nature.

2. In regional demographic analysis, it is important to allow for the possibility that different sorts of activities were carried out at different places in the region. Can artifacts from surface collections made during regional survey be used to monitor such differences in activities? Or is excavation required to make this determination?

If artifact samples recovered by surface collecting are adequate to indicate the relative amounts of artifacts of different periods present in a location, and thus sustain demographic analysis, then the samples can also sustain conclusions about differences in activities in different locations. Both kinds of conclusions are made from samples of artifacts in precisely the same way. In statistical terms the relevant observations take the form of estimates of proportions in a sampling universe on the basis of a sample. The universe that must be characterized is the assemblage of artifacts in a place, however that place is defined. In Chapter 2 we discussed using the proportions of sherds of different periods from surface collections as a way of estimating the amount of garbage deposited in a place during each period. In just the same way, a high proportion of incense burner fragments in a surface collection can indicate greater intensity of ritual activities in that place than in a place where a surface collection yields a lower proportion of incense burner fragments. While much can obviously be learned

from excavations, surface collections may often be more broadly represen-
tative of the overall composition of the artifact assemblage in a place precisely because of the churning and mixing processes that bring artifacts to
the surface, where they can easily be sampled across larger areas than it is
feasible to excavate.

*3. Can maps of changing regional demographic distributions through time enable
us to tell whether local community growth occurs primarily by amalgamation of
multiple communities, in contrast to the dynamics of birth and death rates within
local communities? If so, how?*

Maps of changing demographic distributions do give us insight into
the dynamics of population growth, stasis, and decline at a variety of scales.
The map for one period, for example, may contain a large number of well-
defined, small, low-density artifact scatters. If the map for the succeeding
period shows a small number of well-defined, larger, higher-density artifact scatters, and the overall population proxy for the region differs only
slightly from the previous period, then birth and death rates overall seem
to be in balance—and the conspicuous demographic process playing itself
out would be the formation of larger local communities through the amalgamation of the earlier, smaller communities. By contrast, the maps for the
two periods might be very similar in showing well-defined artifact scatters in pretty much all the same locations. If these were consistently larger
and denser in the second period, then growth of local communities is also
indicated, but through population increase within each one rather than
amalgamation of what were formerly separate local communities.

*4. The units of analysis most often used for rank-size plots in archaeology are sim-
ply sites and the size measured is usually the site area. Does this avoid concerns
about whether sites correspond to local communities?*

The cases in rank-size plots are unavoidably assumed to be meaningful human communities. Archaeological sites as defined in the field can
only be used as the units for rank-size analysis if a convincing case can be
made that there is a good one-to-one correspondence between sites and
local communities. If some single sites really seem better interpreted as
several separate smaller local communities for a particular period, then a
rank-size graph uncritically made of sites as defined in the field will have
one large case that should instead be several much smaller cases. The shape
of the rank-size line will give a very misleading impression of the true pattern of community sizes. A rank-size graph made from sites that should be
combined to better represent local communities will be similarly misleading. And a rank-size graph made from sites that are arbitrary divisions of
an extremely large dispersed scatter of artifacts just for convenience in data
recording will be utterly meaningless.

5. Are the complexities of dealing with demography avoided by making rank-size plots based just on site area?

Most often archaeologists do base rank-size plots on site areas and some have made a particular virtue of this practice, thinking that it avoids problematic issues of demographic reconstruction. The logic of rank-size plots, however, is not about the territory a local community covers but about the relative populations of local communities. Rank-size plots are irreducibly demographic tools. Using site areas to make rank-size plots may be perfectly suitable, but any interpretation is implicitly using area as a population proxy.

6. Does a GIS analysis of the numbers of sites in different environmental zones avoid the complicated assumptions of archaeological demographics?

In a very narrow sense, a GIS analysis of the numbers of sites in different environmental zones can at least pretend to avoid demographic issues. What makes looking at such data interesting and worthwhile, though, is the question of preferences for living in certain environmental zones and the potential reasons for those preferences. For such interpretations it makes a difference if there are many small sites in one zone and fewer but much larger sites in another. The reason this makes a difference is that the two patterns have very different implications about the sizes of local communities and the total numbers of inhabitants in different zones. These are quintessentially demographic implications, so the idea that just focusing on number of sites avoids demography is illusory.

7. Aside from the issue of statistical significance, the result from the Valley of Oax-aca catchment analysis discussed in the last section of this chapter (with its weak but negative correlation) appears to contradict the result from the soil zone analysis (with its stronger and positive correlation). Should we say that in this example from Guadalupe phase Valley of Oaxaca, population distribution does or does not correspond to the distribution of agricultural productivity?

Although the statistical significance of the analysis by soil zones is not as high as we might wish, we can still be nearly 80% confident that people were attracted to at least a moderate extent to live on more productive soils. The catchment analysis tells us that we can be nearly 95% confident that communities with more productive agricultural soils within a 1 km radius did not tend to grow to larger size than others. In fact, the relationship seems to be negative, although it is not very strong. These two conclusions are not really contradictory at all; they are describing different facets of a notoriously multifaceted subject. One might well want to carry out both analyses to answer these two importantly different questions. The question of whether population distribution corresponds to agricultural productivity, then, turns out to be vague and underspecified.

SUGGESTED READINGS

"Together or Apart: The Problem of Nucleation and Dispersal of Settlements" by Bjørn Myhre, in *Settlement and Landscape: Proceedings of a Conference in Århus, Denmark, May 4–7, 1998*, edited by Charlotte Fabech and Jytte Ringtved (Jutland Archaeological Society, Moesgård, Denmark, pp. 125–130, 1999). An exploration of the factors behind living in compact, nucleated villages or dispersed farmsteads in a Scandinavian context.

"Residential Ethnoarchaeology and Ancient Site Structure: Contemporary Farming and Prehistoric Settlement Agriculture at Matacapan, Veracruz, Mexico" by Thomas W. Killion, in *Gardens of Prehistory: The Archaeology of Settlement Agriculture in Greater Mesoamerica* edited by Thomas W. Killion (University of Alabama Press, Tuscaloosa, pp. 119–149, 1992). Cultivation in the spaces between relatively dispersed households, its relationship to surface artifact densities, and its connection to regional-scale survey data.

"Interaction Structures and the Development of Early Complex Society in Southern Central America and Northern South America" by C. Adam Berrey, in *Multiscalar Approaches to Studying Social Organization in the Isthmo-Colombian Area* edited by Scott D. Palumbo, Ana María Boada Rivas, William A. Locascio, and Adam C. J. Menzies (Center for Comparative Archaeology, University of Pittsburgh, pp. 1–14, 2013). Explores the developmental implications of compact, nucleated local communities versus dispersed farmstead living.

"Agrarian Features, Farmsteads, and Homesteads in the Río Bec Nuclear Zone, Mexico" by Eva Lemonier and Boris Vennière (*Ancient Mesoamerica* 24:397–413, 2013). Argues for autonomous farmstead organization of agricultural production among the Classic Maya.

"Sea Changes in Stable Communities: What Do Small Changes in Practices at Çatalhöyük and Chiripa Imply about Community Making?" by Christine A. Hastorf, in *Becoming Villagers: Comparing Early Village Societies* edited by Matthew S. Bandy and Jake R. Fox (University of Arizona Press, Tucson, pp. 140–161, 2010). Identity, social interaction, and changing views of one's place in the world in compact, nucleated local communities.

"Jiangzhai: Social and Economic Organization in a Middle Neolithic Chinese Village" by Christian E. Peterson and Gideon Shelach (*Journal of Anthropological Archaeology* 31:265–301, 2012). Subsistence and non-subsistence production, privatization and accumulation of resources, kinship, and social segmentation in a compact, nucleated local community.

"Communities, Settlements, Sites, and Surveys: Regional-Scale Analysis of Prehistoric Human Interaction" by Christian E. Peterson and Robert D. Drennan (*American Antiquity* 70:5–30, 2005). A theoretical and methodological consideration of distance-interaction principles, compact versus dispersed settlement, and regional-scale settlement clustering.

"A Reconstruction of Toltec Period Political Units in the Valley of Mexico" by John R. Alden, in *Transformations: Mathematical Approaches to Culture Change* edited by Colin Renfrew and Kenneth L. Cooke (Academic Press, New York, pp. 169–200, 1979). Distance-interaction principles are used to delineate settlement clusters separated by buffer zones. The interpretation of both Aztec and Toltec clusters as polities is bolstered by ethnohistorical information for Aztec times.

"Modeling and Testing Polity Boundaries in the Classic Tuxtla Mountains, Southern Veracruz, Mexico" by Wesley D. Stoner (*Journal of Anthropological Archaeology* 31:381–402, 2012). Regional polity boundaries delineated according to distance-interaction and other principles.

Settlement and Politics in Three Classic Maya Polities by Olivier de Montmollin (Prehistory Press, Madison, WI, 1995). Polity capitals and territories delineated with multiple criteria, especially emphasizing surface remains of architecture. Elite and commoner populations are distinguished and their distributions analyzed in detail with respect to the spatial organization of polities.

"Comparing Archaeological Settlement Systems with Rank-Size Graphs: A Measure of Shape and Statistical Confidence" by Robert D. Drennan and Christian E. Peterson (*Journal of Archaeological Science* 31:533–549, 2004). Advantages and disadvantages of rank-size graphs, the A coefficient to characterize their shape, and comparative examples.

"Centralized Communities, Population, and Social Complexity after Sedentarization" by Robert D. Drennan and Christian E. Peterson, in *The Neolithic Demographic Transition and Its Consequences* edited by Jean-Pierre Bocquet-Appel and Ofer Bar-Yosef (Springer-Verlag, New York, pp. 359–386, 2008). The B coefficient to measure the strength and significance of centralization on the basis of the distribution of population in a series of concentric rings.

"Some Recent Data and Concepts about Ancient Urbanism" by George L. Cowgill, in *Urbanism in Mesoamerica, Vol. 1,* edited by William T. Sanders, Alba Guadalupe Mastache, and Robert H. Cobean (Instituto Nacional de Antropología e Historia, Mexico City, and Pennsylvania State University, University Park, pp. 1–19, 2003). Includes a discussion of the unsound practice of identifying the number of tiers in a settlement hierarchy by examining site size histograms.

Monte Albán's Hinterland, Part I: The Prehispanic Settlement Patterns of the Central and Southern Parts of the Valley of Oaxaca, Mexico by Richard E. Blanton, Stephen A. Kowalewski, Gary M. Feinman, and Jill Appel (Memoirs of the University of Michigan Museum of Anthropology, No. 15, 1982) and *Monte Albán's Hinterland, Part II: Prehispanic Settlement Patterns in Tlacolula, Etla, and Ocotlán, the Valley of Oaxaca, Mexico* by Stephen A. Kowalewski, Gary M. Feinman, Laura Finsten, Richard E. Blanton, and Linda M. Nicholas (Memoirs of the University of Michigan Museum of Anthropology, No. 23, 1989). Examples in this and subsequent chapters draw heavily on data and analyses from the Valley of Oaxaca survey.

Geographical Information Systems in Archaeology by James Conolly and Mark Lake (Cambridge University Press, Cambridge, UK, 2006). A broad introduction to the use of GIS tools for analyses like those discussed in this chapter, among others.

CHAPTER 4

HOW CAN WE ESTIMATE ABSOLUTE NUMBERS OF INHABITANTS?

Estimating absolute numbers of inhabitants is often the first step in regional settlement analysis, since it seems superficially that this provides the necessary basis for all the other analyses that follow. This is not an unreasonable attitude, but we have deviated from this practice in order to emphasize that quite a lot of regional demographic analysis in archaeology can be accomplished with the relative estimates provided directly by archaeological population proxies that are taken to be proportional to the absolute numbers of inhabitants. The issues raised in Chapter 3 can all be addressed with population proxies; estimates of absolute numbers are not needed.

This observation matters because converting archaeological population proxies into estimates of absolute numbers is the most error-prone part of regional settlement demography. We can be much more confident when we say that one local community had about twice as many inhabitants as another than when we say that one local community had about 300 inhabitants and another, about 150. This is ubiquitously recognized and absolute numbers are often stated in terms of minimum and maximum estimates that may differ quite substantially. The fact that we can be more confident of the relative estimates provided by population proxies means that analyses that really depend only on population proxies produce more reliable results than those that require absolute numbers. The analytical subjects discussed in Chapter 3, then, are on a more solid footing because they are not subject to the additional kinds of error that come with estimating absolute numbers—the subject of this chapter.

If estimating absolute numbers of inhabitants is so fraught with error, we should re-ask the question from the first chapter in this more limited context: "Why bother?" We have seen in Chapter 3 that many enlightening conclusions about ancient societies can be based on population proxies.

Why not just leave it at that? It is worth facing the risks of estimating absolute numbers because it enables us to go beyond what we can do with population proxies alone.

Chapter 3 dealt with the importance of delineating local communities, to enable us to reconstruct ancient interaction structures and give us the social units we need for further analysis. The demographic scale of a local community has implications for the social relations that develop within it and with neighboring communities. Categories of local communities—like hamlet, village, town, and city—imply different absolute demographic scales, and the social dynamics of hamlets, villages, towns, and cities are quite different as a consequence of this difference in scale (among other things). There are implications even for what we think of as more purely mental processes: people's sense of who they are and how they fit into a world populated by other people. In fact, the longstanding practice of imagining sites as hamlets, villages, and the like carries us squarely into the arena of absolute numbers of inhabitants; it just does it surreptitiously without actually mentioning the numbers. Making the numbers explicit enhances our ability to evaluate and improve the methods used and to assess realistically how confident we should be of the results. Absolute numbers can also add a layer of meaning to analyses of demographic distributions in relation to resource distributions, by providing an approximate account of resource surpluses or deficits in particular places or regions.

COUNTING HOUSES

In Chapter 2 we considered the possibility of counting house structures (see Figure 2.1), or even individual rooms within structures, to arrive at a regional-scale population proxy. In principle, converting such a population proxy into an absolute population estimate is not difficult; it simply requires determining how many people, on average, lived in a house structure or room. Several worldwide averages for the number of people per square meter of roofed area in house structures, based on ethnographic data, have been published. These have sometimes been used, in conjunction with data from excavated house structures in the region, if excavation is needed for determining house areas. It has been observed that these worldwide averages mask the quite considerable variation that occurs from region to region in the ethnographic data, giving an illusory sense of both confidence and precision. For some regions there is ethnographic information for groups closely related to archaeological settlements, and the particular figures for these groups can be used in place of global averages. Finally, these sources of information typically converge on dividing the average roofed area of houses for the region and period by the average number of square meters per person, and multiplying the result by the number of houses counted to arrive at an absolute population estimate.

A slightly different approach involves making a case that individual house structures are nuclear family residences because, for example, they seem too big to house only one or two people (which would be an unusual residential pattern ethnographically in any event) and too small for extended families consisting, say, of two or more sisters and their husbands and children. Then some average number of people per nuclear family is chosen and multiplied by the number of houses to arrive at an absolute population estimate. The average number of people per nuclear family can be drawn from global ethnographic averages, or from more closely related groups for which ethnographic information is available. The absolute population estimate is the number of houses counted, multiplied by the average number of members of a nuclear family. Sometimes variation in the number of members of a nuclear family forms the intuitive basis for minimum and maximum population estimates. The number of houses might be multiplied by, say, four (as a minimum average number for a nuclear family) to produce an overall minimum population estimate, and by seven (as a maximum average number for a nuclear family) for an overall maximum population estimate.

In instances where house structures themselves cannot be observed on the surface, other domestic features may be. The residential locations of individual households can sometimes be identified as concentrations of artifacts on the surface that result from garbage disposal in the immediate vicinity of the house structure. Detailed recording of surface artifact distributions can sometimes reveal quite clearly the location of the house structure in an area of relatively low artifact density (floors, after all, are normally kept clean) surrounded by a ring of higher artifact densities where garbage disposal in the area around—and especially behind—the house created midden deposits (Figure 4.1). Such surface traces of individual household locations are not restricted to relatively recent periods. They can persist through many millennia, even in intensively used landscapes, and make it possible to count households and map their spacing and distribution through local communities (Figure 4.2).

A seldom-considered but potentially important concern for those estimating populations from an average family size is that when demographic growth results from shifts in birth and death rates, the average size of the nuclear family increases. This is seldom taken into account in regional settlement demography, which would not entirely invalidate the absolute population estimates, although it might lead to an understatement of growth episodes. Since average nuclear family size would decrease when population declines from either increasing death rates or decreasing birth rates, episodes of population decline might also be understated. These issues of changes through time in average family size (or in average number

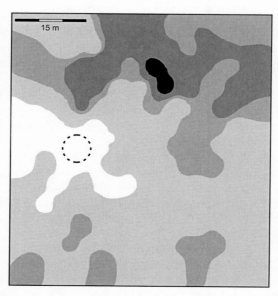

Figure 4.1. Density contours showing ring of higher artifact densities surrounding an Early Muisca (800–1200 AD) house in the Sabana de Bogotá, Colombia. Darker areas have higher densities; dashed line is the probable location of a house structure in a low-density patch that would include exterior activity areas as well. The low-density pathway toward the left seems likely to be the entrance. (Data from Kruschek 2003:102.)

of occupants per house), however, can in principle be allowed for by using data on changing house size from excavations at a few sites or on changing age structure of a population from excavated cemeteries, as discussed in Chapter 2.

The impact of several other factors—ones that we largely set aside in talking about counting houses as a population proxy—could be more severe. Contemporaneity of the houses counted and their year-round occupation did not have to be determined in using house counts as a relative population proxy; we simply had to be confident that these things were the same for the settlements, periods, or regions involved. If house counts are the basis of absolute population estimates, however, both issues must be addressed head-on.

Since the periods that provide the best chronological control we have in regional settlement analysis are often long, it is very likely that some or all of the houses we count were occupied for only a part of the total time span. To the extent that this is the case, counting houses will overestimate the population. Determining true contemporaneity of occupation for house

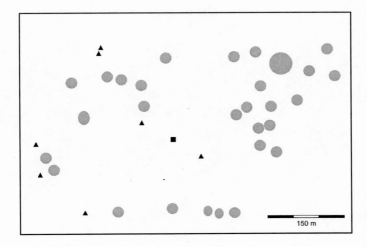

Figure 4.2. Locations of households (gray) as indicated by high-density artifact hotspots at the small dispersed Hongshan (4500–3000 BC) village of Fushanzhuang. Black square locates the remains of an elaborate burial; black triangles are the remains of platforms. (Data from Peterson 2006:194.)

structures across an entire region is seldom feasible. The average lifetime of a house structure, however, might be estimated if a sufficient amount of data from excavated house structures at a few sites are available (and especially if these data include abundant chronometric dates). The total number of houses counted in the region could then be divided by the average lifetime of a house to produce a more reliable absolute population estimate for the region (or for a sector of it, or for particular local communities, etc.).

Following a course like this assumes that the number of houses counted is indeed the total number of house structures built during the period—that is, that none were ever destroyed. It would usually be difficult to justify this assumption. A case can be made, though, for example, for a wet tropical region, such as the lowland Maya area, where the count is not actually of house structures but of house mounds, each of which is likely to represent a near continuous sequence of structures one after another.

If the population of a region moves back and forth semi-annually, say between two parts of the region, counting houses will estimate twice the true population. If the population moves semi-annually in and out of the study region, counting houses is a more direct route to estimating the number of inhabitants, at least for the season when they are there. Such a seasonal pattern of occupation can of course be revealed through such things as plant and animal remains that indicate seasonality, which can be recovered from excavations at a few sites to characterize the pattern.

Figure 4.3. Large area of excavated residential structures at the heavily fortified Lower Xiajiadian (2000–1200 BC) site of Sanzuodian, China.

In principle, then, counting houses can provide a sound basis for estimating the absolute number of inhabitants at a regional scale, although there are more potentially confounding factors than initially meet the eye. The more data are available from careful excavation of house structures for determining regionally specific procedures and practices, the more confidence we can have in such reconstructions, although the resources needed to excavate large areas of residential sites are not always easy to come by (Figure 4.3). The broadest limitation to this approach is that the nature of the archaeological record for most places does not make it possible to count house structures across a region, because they do not systematically leave sufficiently visible surface remains. Even a few unusual sites in a region where individual households are identifiable, either from excavations or on the surface, can nonetheless provide a crucial link between population estimates based on household counts and population proxies of more practical utility at a regional scale.

MEASURING AREAS OF LOCAL COMMUNITIES

In Chapter 2 we concluded that the area occupied may have a sufficiently consistent relationship to the number of inhabitants to be used as a reliable population proxy in at least some regions. Usually this means that the internal density of occupation is relatively consistent across the local communities in a region, although the principle can also work well for dispersed farmsteads in a distribution that lacks a local community structure. As we also discussed in Chapter 2, more densely or intensively occupied areas are usually indicated by higher densities of archaeological materials. Thus, if the density of archaeological materials varies little across the places where they are present, area by itself may well provide a serviceable population proxy.

It is unsettling when the decision to use occupied area as a population proxy is reached solely on the grounds that modern surface conditions make it difficult to measure the density of remains. It is certainly true that modern occupation or land use, the nature of vegetation cover, and other factors can affect the apparent density of surface artifacts, sometimes quite dramatically. Where this is the case, it is still usually possible (and worthwhile) to assess densities in a reduced number of places—where this can be done convincingly—in order to determine whether they seem consistently low, consistently high, or highly variable.

In the Valle de la Plata, vegetation made convincing assessment of densities impossible in conditions ranging from cleared cattle pasture covered with dense grass to heavy tropical montane forest. In fact, these conditions made it impossible in some locations to determine even whether artifacts were present or not simply by inspecting the surface. In such locations surface collections were replaced by shovel probes, a technique we will discuss further in Chapter 5. The shovel probes were of a consistent size, so densities were quantified wherever shovel probes were dug. In most places surface collections were relied upon (because they are much quicker than shovel probes), but this meant no reliable assessment of densities for those places because of variable vegetation cover.

Both the general impression conveyed by surface collections and the sherd counts from shovel probes indicated that average densities of materials in the Valle de la Plata were quite low: less than about 2 sherds/m^2 in the vast majority of cases. A small number of shovel probes, however, revealed much higher densities—raising the possibility that at least a few densely settled local communities might be overlooked if sherd densities were simply assumed to be ubiquitously low and area were used by itself as a population proxy. The spatial distribution of shovel probes with high densities of sherds provided a clue that this last possibility was not a worry. If the high-density shovel probes did reflect a few high-density local communities, they would have clustered in the locations of those communities. Instead they were broadly scattered across the entire survey zone; no two were contiguous and no more than three ever occurred in a space as small as 1 km^2.

A better interpretation of the high-density shovel probes is that they happened by pure chance to encounter extremely concentrated but very local midden deposits. This phenomenon has been observed in larger-scale excavations as well; sherd densities of astronomical proportions are occasionally encountered in an area as small as 2 or 3 m^2 in association with a single house structure with no near neighbors. The shovel probes, then, provided an argument that sherd densities in the Valle de la Plata could be taken as consistently low and area could serve as a reliable population proxy. Strictly speaking, if an argument like this is made, it is not accurate to say that sherd densities have been disregarded in favor of area as the population proxy. In practical terms, though, the density value is treated as a constant, so it disappears and the calculation of the population proxy is as if density had not been considered.

Converting area into an estimate of absolute numbers is usually a question of establishing the average number of inhabitants per unit of archaeologically measured area of occupation—that is, the number of people per hectare within settlements. Sometimes census data are used for this purpose. If the latter part of the archaeological sequence studied comes close enough to periods for which census data are available, and the form of settlement for the late archaeological periods is very much like the form of settlement for periods with census data, then this connection can be convincing. Even when the time gap is longer, comparing data from a few excavated sites with ethnographic observations may convince us that the nature and spacing of houses within settlements is quite similar between archaeological periods and more recent periods with census data, and enable us to use residential densities from ethnographic information to convert area measurements into estimates of absolute population.

Census data for the city of Erbil, in Iraq, were used in early regional settlement demography. Because the nature and spacing of houses within Erbil seemed similar to those documented in excavations of Mesopotamian tells, the number of inhabitants per hectare in Erbil was extrapolated to a range of 100–200 inhabitants/ha to serve as the basis for calculating population estimates of ancient Mesopotamian cities based on their areas in different periods. For the Rizhao region of eastern China, census data for contemporary traditional villages and measurements of their areas yielded an average of 72.2 persons/ha. This figure was multiplied by archaeologically documented occupied areas for Longshan, Zhou, and Han times (2600 BC–220 AD) to arrive at population estimates for these periods. The issue of just how precise these estimates are was not considered, but widespread practice in regional settlement demography would often take an average like 72.2 persons/ha as hyper-precise and use a range of 50–100 persons/ha for multiplying by archaeological areas to provide minimum and maximum absolute population estimates—thus conveying a sense of how precise the estimates were believed to be.

Confounding Factors

Area is probably the population proxy most often converted into absolute population estimates, and this is usually done in the manner just described by multiplying occupied area by an average number of inhabitants per hectare derived from ethnographic and/or census data. The subject of whether that average number of inhabitants per hectare varies considerably from place to place within a region is seldom the subject of much scrutiny, making this common practice somewhat more risky than it really needs to be. A critical examination of the data used to establish an average number of persons per hectare might lead to ways to reduce the error in the population estimates made.

A brief example of the benefits to be derived from a careful look at the data comes from the Carhuarazo Valley in highland Peru. Population data are available for 11 small settlements from a census taken in 1540, and the occupied areas of the corresponding 11 archaeological sites could be measured accurately because their inhabitants were forcibly moved to new locations by Spanish colonial administrators soon after 1540. The correlation between population and occupied area is strong and highly significant ($r = 0.905$, $p < 0.0005$, $n = 11$). As in the case of the modern examples we looked at in Chapter 2, however, the scatterplot shows an outlier that has excessive influence on this result (Figure 4.4). When this outlier is removed (Figure 4.4), the results are discouraging. Although the sample is large enough to give us 85% confidence, the correlation is markedly weakened ($r = 0.488$, $p = 0.152$, $n = 10$). Since only about 24% of the variation in population is accounted for by occupied area, one should hesitate to use area as a population proxy or, needless to say, to convert it into an absolute population estimate, because the resulting estimate would not be at all reliable—that is to say, it would come with an extremely wide error range.

The positive outcome of this examination was the observation that three different categories of settlements could be recognized. There were

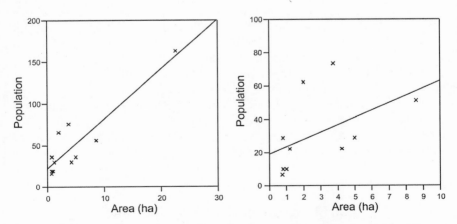

Figure 4.4. Scatterplots of archaeologically measured occupied area and 16th century census population for nucleated local communities in the Carhuarazo Valley, including (left) and excluding (right) the high outlier of Apcara. (Data from Schrieber and Kintigh 1996:573–579.)

central places, ordinary villages, and ordinary villages in topographically constrained locations. Once the already small sample was divided into these three categories, there were very few examples of each, but it did seem that ordinary villages had fairly consistent occupational densities of 20–30 persons/ha. Central places also had fairly consistent densities, but lower—less than 10 persons/ha, probably attributable to the greater use of space for open public areas and other special functions. And villages in topographically constrained locations had densities consistently above 30 persons/ha, presumably because they were crowded into tight spaces by their settings.

In this case, then, where using area as a population proxy did not initially seem promising, the situation could be improved by paying attention to what would turn up in the archaeological record as "site types," each of which had a relatively consistent occupational density but not the same density as the other types. It was also observed that this variation in density across different types of settlements could be characterized reasonably well as a nonlinear relationship. An even better result might be obtained by incorporating the density of archaeological remains into the calculation (see below).

Two more factors confounding the conversion of area into absolute population estimates are contemporaneity and possible seasonality of occupation. These factors operate on calculations of area exactly as they do on counts of houses and both were discussed in the preceding section. If residential areas were occupied during only half a chronological period by people who lived elsewhere in the region during the other half of the time, then populations would be double-counted. This could take the form of an area occupied for the first half of the period by people who lived elsewhere in the region during the second half of the period (or whose descendants did). Or, alternatively, it could be a question of seasonal occupations by people who lived in one place for six months each year and elsewhere in the region for the rest of the year. In either case the outcome would be the same: inhabitants are counted twice if population estimates are based strictly on area occupied. This potential source of error may not seriously affect relative population estimates through time if this aspect of residence patterns remains constant. It will, however, always affect absolute population estimates based on occupied area alone. Incorporating the density of archaeological remains into the calculation along with area can help cope with such issues.

COMBINING DENSITY WITH AREA

Area and density of surface scatters were first systematically used together as a basis for regional settlement demography in the Basin of Mexico. As discussed in Chapter 2, each of several density categories (in sherds/m²) was assigned a corresponding occupational density (in persons/hectare). All the occupational densities were stated as ranges between a minimum and maximum estimate, reflecting the degree of precision the estimates were considered to have. A moderate surface sherd density estimated at 100–200 sherds/m^2, for example, was assigned an occupational density of 25–50 persons/ha. (It may be worth noting that 100–200 sherds/m^2 would be almost incredibly high for many regions.) For each occupied area—or part of an occupied area—then, a number of inhabitants was assigned (actually a range between a minimum and maximum estimate) based on how much area it covered and how dense the surface sherds of a particular period were. These estimated numbers of inhabitants were then added up for each local community or other residential area, and those results were summed for larger parts of the region and eventually for the entire Basin. The number of inhabitants per hectare assigned to each sherd density category was based on several different kinds of information.

For some residential areas dating to the Aztec period (the last before the Spanish Conquest), house foundations were well preserved and visible on the surface so that houses could be counted. Their density within occupied areas varied from 1 or 2 houses/ha up to 20 houses/ha, and this density corresponded well with the density of surface sherds of Aztec times (in sherds/m^2). This provided an estimate of how many families, and thus people, per hectare corresponded to different sherd density categories. This estimate was further refined by observations of the numbers of houses per hectare in modern villages of relatively traditional form in rural sectors of the Basin of Mexico.

The resulting population estimates were then checked in two ways. The first started with the earliest Spanish Colonial period censuses, dating to around 1560. These were projected back to 1519, the peak of pre-Hispanic population for Aztec times in the Basin of Mexico when the Spanish first arrived. This projection had to allow, primarily, for the population decline that had already occurred as a consequence of the introduction of European diseases. In the end the 1519 population estimates derived from historic censuses were about 20% higher than the maximum estimates derived from the archaeological remains, as described above.

The second check was based on extensive excavations of residential sites from early in the Basin of Mexico sequence. These sites spanned much of the Formative period (1500–300 BC). El Arbolillo, Zacatenco, and Ticomán were excavated early in the 20th century; Loma Torremote was excavated in 1974 as part of the Basin of Mexico project. For El Arbolillo, Zacatenco, and Ticomán there were large samples of burials and relatively tight chronology, so estimates were built on a calculation of the local population sizes that would produce the numbers of deaths documented by the burial data. The same was done for Loma Torremote and the number and spacing of house compounds also produced a population estimate.

Agreement between these population estimates and those derived from surface remains (as described above) was better in some instances than in others. The overall trend, though, was similar to that observed in the analysis of historic census data: population estimates from surface archaeological remains were about 20% lower than those based on the two classes of excavated information—about the same discrepancy noted between the population estimates from surface remains and those projected back from Colonial period censuses. Some will surely think this discrepancy distressing; we are much more inclined to agree with Sanders and his colleagues in the Basin of Mexico research and characterize it as a "remarkable level of agreement."

The residential densities in people per hectare assigned to particular surface artifact density categories in the Basin of Mexico might apply in other regions as well, although there is no reason to believe that they necessarily will. The same approach to using both area and density of remains to make absolute population estimates was used, for example, for the Tonosí Valley in Panama. The equivalence between sherd density categories and residential density categories was based on counted households and artifact densities at excavated sites. The numbers were similar to those arrived at in the Basin of Mexico, but not identical.

The Area-Density Index

The area-density index discussed in Chapter 2 does comprise a relative population proxy entirely separate from considerations of absolute numbers of inhabitants. How to convert it into an absolute estimate thus arises clearly as a subsequent question. It is useful to remember that the area-density index was suggested as a way to quantify the amount of garbage deposited on the landscape in a place or region during a particular period. Thinking of it in this way helps make clear how converting it into an absolute population estimate can be approached, as well as just how the resulting absolute population estimate can be interpreted.

As calculated in Chapter 2, the area-density index is the surface density of sherds of a particular period (in sherds/m^2) multiplied by the area covered (in hectares). One unit in the area-density index is thus equivalent to a surface density of 1 sherd/m^2 across an area of 1 ha. In population terms one unit in the area-density index is equivalent to the number of people whose garbage, deposited during a particular period, would produce an archaeological artifact scatter covering 1 ha with sherds of that period at a density of 1 sherd/m^2. The area-density index assumes that this same number of people might live closer together and deposit their garbage over 0.5 ha, resulting in a sherd scatter with a density of 2 sherds/m^2.

This behavior of the area-density index obviates some of the worries discussed above that adhere to estimates based on area alone. Concern, for example, about site types occupied at different residential densities disappears. The different occupational densities observed at three site types in the Carhuarazo Valley would be reflected in higher surface artifact densities at villages in topographically constrained locations, lower surface artifact densities at normal villages, and still lower surface densities at centers whose measured areas would include large open public spaces. It would thus not be necessary to classify sites into these types and apply different calculations to each to estimate populations, but only to multiply the higher densities of villages in topographically constrained areas by their smaller areas to arrive at population estimates compatible with those for larger but sparser normal villages.

As discussed in Chapter 2, archaeological periods often vary substantially in length, so it is usually convenient to divide the area-density index by the number of centuries in the period in question to allow for the fact that the same number of people will deposit more garbage during longer periods, resulting in larger areas covered and/or higher surface densities of artifacts.

Magic Numbers

Finally, the "magic number" we're looking for is the number of people whose garbage accumulated over 1 century will on average leave an archaeological sherd scatter of 1 sherd/m^2 across an area of 1 ha. No one number will be valid for all times and places; it must be established anew for each region and it may well change through the time sequence studied in a particular region. The principal route to establishing this number for a particular context goes by way of a sample of archaeological sites for which it is possible to connect the area and density of surface remains with an estimate of the number of inhabitants derived from other sources of information—the kind of information it is usually possible to collect for very small areas but not for entire regions. This is the route pioneered by research in the Basin of Mexico.

The array of possibilities for making absolute estimates of population at a small scale is quite broad. One, of course, is to use actual head counts in the form of modern or historic censuses and we have already explored this option in connection with area as a population proxy. The actual process of fitting all the necessary pieces together may be quite complicated. It may be a challenge to project census data back to a time period when they can be correlated with archaeological sites, as it was for the Basin of Mexico. It may be a challenge to identify the archaeological sites corresponding to local communities that appear in census data, although it wasn't for the Carhuarazo Valley. But the principle is straightforward.

If the census populations for a series of communities are fairly consistently about 50 times the area-density index values calculated for the corresponding archaeological sites, then multiplying the area-density index by 50 will yield a reasonably accurate absolute population estimate for sites of that period and region. If the relationship is less consistent, but census populations regularly fall between about 35 and 65 times the corresponding area-density index values, then the area-density index might reasonably be multiplied by 35 for a minimum absolute population estimate and 65 for a maximum. If the number of cases is sufficient, a finer point can of course be put on this relationship with a regression analysis. The equation for the best-fit line might provide the most appropriate mathematical tool for calculating the estimate, and would also make it possible to establish an error range (that is, minimum and maximum estimates) for a statistically determined confidence level. This has not yet been done for an area-density index (largely for lack of a sufficient number of cases) but regression analysis was a fruitful approach to the Carhuarazo Valley site areas discussed above.

Using archaeologically based population estimates for a sample of local communities to establish the absolute population equivalents of area-density index values is especially appealing, because this practice can provide powerful help in guarding against the series of "other things being equal" assumptions discussed in Chapter 2. Such an approach does, however, place heavy demands on the available documentation of the archaeological record. Ideally, a large number of sites dating to various periods in or near the region being studied will have been extensively excavated or comprehensively sampled. Structures, features, and artifacts will have been recorded and described—both qualitatively and quantitatively—and the detailed results will be available for analysis, typically because they have been published. A body of information like this will make it possible to estimate the absolute population for each excavated site. Finally, detailed quantitative information will be wanted on the area and density of surface artifacts on the site prior to excavation.

This last provides the key link for connecting the absolute population estimates for excavated sites to the area-density index, and it is the category of information most often lacking from otherwise detailed excavation reports. This omission is likely to stem from the assumption at the outset of a major excavation project that much more detailed information will be forthcoming from the excavations about to begin, and there is thus no need to record anything about the artifacts on the surface. This is a shame, since systematic recording of the area and density of surface artifacts prior to excavation could be accomplished quite quickly and could be used to greatly enhance the reliability and precision of regional settlement demography.

The Chifeng region, where the area-density index described here was first used, better satisfies these demands for the availability of ancillary information from excavated sites than many regions do—although a considerable amount of educated guessing was still necessary. Linking the area-density index for Chifeng to absolute population estimates began with a graphical summary of the area-density values produced by the Chifeng regional survey across an area of 1,234 km² and including periods spanning the time from about 6000 BC to 1300 AD. These values covered quite a wide range for each period, although the high values for some periods were much higher than for others (Figure 4.5). The upper ends of the lines representing the ranges in Figure 4.5 are broken to reflect the fact that high outliers were omitted so that the ranges as represented in the graph would more usefully reflect the batches of numbers.

As graphed in Figure 4.5, the area-density values have already been divided by the number of centuries in the corresponding periods. Next ab-

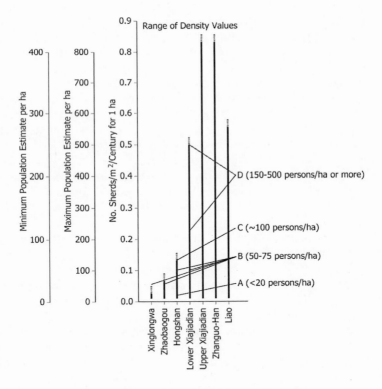

Figure 4.5. Ranges of area-density values recorded for collection units in Chifeng for each period in the sequence. Letters indicate sites for which absolute population estimates could be made by counting houses, located in the positions they belong in on the scale of area-density values for their periods. Scales for maximum and minimum population estimates have been added to match the population estimates for excavated sites. (Data from Chifeng 2011a:72–78, 2011b.)

solute population estimates were compiled for sites in and around the Chifeng region where extensive excavations or surface remains made it possible to count contemporaneous house structures. Educated guesses had to be made in most cases about the areas and densities of surface artifacts that characterized these sites prior to excavation, although more systematic information was available for some. The education of these guesses included the informal recollections of the excavators of some sites.

These sites were then placed in appropriate positions in the density ranges for their respective periods according to the educated guesses about their surfaces prior to excavation. Excavated sites in the lower density ranges are particularly scarce because archaeologists seldom choose to excavate small sites with remains that are sparse for their period. (The fact that extensively excavated sites are mostly the larger and denser ones creates a sampling bias that has a strong and often unrecognized impact on our conclusions about patterns of organization and life in general in the prehistoric past.) One Hongshan period site, however, indicated by A in Figure 4.5, did fall in this low artifact density range; actually this is a relatively ephemeral occupation at a site excavated primarily because of its denser occupation in a different period. Several sites with somewhat higher artifact densities (B in Figure 4.5) fell near the top of the scale for the Xinglongwa and Zhaobaogou periods, a bit below the top of the scale for Hongshan, and in a relatively low position for Lower Xiajiadian—whose sites often have very much higher densities than any that had occurred previously. At still higher artifact density levels, the site labeled C in Figure 4.5 fell near the top of the scale for Hongshan times. And finally, several heavily fortified Early Bronze Age sites varied substantially in density and were spread through the upper half of the scale for Lower Xiajiadian times.

The last step in the process was to use the absolute population estimates for these sites, which had already been positioned in the area-density graph according to their densities, to affix an absolute population scale to the graph (Figure 4.5). This was done in such a way as to bracket the best-estimate pattern with minimum and maximum values as a reminder of the fairly low level of precision of these estimates. Once these scales are positioned, it is easy to determine that multiplying the area-density index on the original scale by 500 produces the numbers on the minimum population estimate scale, and multiplying them by 1000 produces the numbers on the maximum population estimate scale. These, then, are the "magic numbers" we were looking for to convert an area-density index into an absolute population estimate for the Chifeng region. We emphasize again that very different numbers have been convincingly arrived at for other regions; these are not universal constants.

There is sufficient redundancy of sites with different area-density values and population estimates, to provide reassurance for the first four periods across the range of area-density values represented for this earlier part of the sequence. That is, there are enough sites that contradictions could well have arisen; the fact that they did not enhances confidence in the outcome. The same cannot be said for the last three periods or for the upper parts of their area-density ranges, which extend substantially above values seen in the first four periods. There were no sites for which independent absolute population estimates could be made, meaning that the conversion scale has been extended considerably beyond the range of the points upon which it was based, both in terms of area-density values and in terms of time periods. This makes the estimates less reliable for the latter part of the sequence than for the earlier part, but a conversion has been arrived at that provides a way to convert an area-density value into an absolute population estimate for any collection unit, local community, supra-local community, or any other sector of the Chifeng region.

To the extent that this conversion is based on separate area-density values and absolute population estimates for sites of different periods, it automatically helps to compensate for some of the "other things being equal" issues discussed in Chapter 2. For instance, the conversion implicitly takes into account that rates of ceramic use per person may have changed through time, because the correspondence between area-density values and absolute population numbers was based for each period on sites of that period (at whatever rate of ceramic use per person obtained during that period). This aspect of the conversion in particular would be much more reliable if there had been more excavated sites for each period and less educated guessing in establishing area-density values for excavated sites.

It is not at all difficult, conceptually, to increase reliability in this way. It does not even require imagining unimaginable sums of money for extensive excavation at large numbers of sites. Many more sites, actually, have already been excavated. Only two elements are lacking, and they are also not costly or conceptually challenging elements. First, the results of many potentially useful excavation projects have not been published or otherwise made available (or not published in enough detail to be useful for these purposes). And second, very few archaeologists are in the habit of collecting and publishing systematic information about the area and density of surface remains before they began to excavate.

We hasten to add that this is not in particular a characterization of the Chifeng region; there is no part of the world to which it is not applicable. Greater vigor in the publication of results and attention to this one detail by a larger number of field archaeologists would make possible the accumulation of a much larger and more reliable basis for regional settlement demography, much in the way that radiocarbon chronologies have slowly accumulated for most regions with the addition of one or two or five dates from a multitude of sites as they were excavated.

Ex Post Facto Checks

Whatever the means of converting a population proxy into an absolute population estimate, the approach can be verified, corrected, or invalidated by ex post facto checking. This generally involves looking for other lines of evidence that will either converge or not with the absolute population estimates already made. To the extent that additional lines of evidence tend to converge with the estimates, we should have greater confidence in them. If additional lines of evidence lead to rather different results, then our confidence should diminish.

The Rizhao population estimates discussed above, for example, which were based on contemporary settlements and census data, were compared with the results of a Han census taken in 2 AD. This census had very little detail but counted 1,079,100 inhabitants (a density of about 50 persons/km^2) in Langya Province, which included the Rizhao survey area. At 50 persons/km^2 the Rizhao survey area should have had 20,000 inhabitants. Using minimum and maximum figures, the Rizhao area had an archaeologically estimated population of 42,000–84,000, or 2–4 times the estimate based on the provincial population density from the Han census. This apparent discrepancy, however, may actually represent quite good agreement since the province includes highly varied terrain and soils of very different agricultural productivity. It is to be expected that the largely agrarian population would be more concentrated in areas of high agricultural productivity, and that is exactly what the Rizhao survey area was. A population density 2–4 times the average for Langya Province, then, seems not unreasonable at all.

Demographic calculations in the Alto Magdalena were based on uniform low sherd densities that were estimated to correspond to 1–2 households/ha (or 5–10 persons/ha). More intensive investigation of the central community of Mesitas revealed concentrations of artifacts that appeared to correspond to 68 relatively dispersed individual Regional Classic household locations. Since Mesitas was included in the Alto Magdalena regional survey, this result could be compared with the regional survey result. The areas of occupation corresponding to the 68 household locations were measured in the regional survey at 37.7 ha, yielding an average of 1.8 households/ha.

There is reason to believe that this number is abnormally high for the Valle de la Plata since Mesitas includes one small group of households unusually close together. If this group of households is excluded, the average drops to 1.4 households/ha. Both numbers are, in any event, within the range of 1–2 households/ha upon which the Alto Magdalena population estimates were based. Yet another ex post facto check on Alto Magdalena population estimates began with ethnoarchaeological observation to determine the mean area of garbage distribution around modern dispersed farmsteads. Circles of this mean area were drawn around the locations of all modern dispersed farmsteads in the municipality that corresponds roughly to the archaeological survey zone. This was taken as a map of the artifact scatters that the modern rural population distribution would produce if recorded archaeologically. The total occupied area of 776 ha corresponded to 946 households, for an average of 1.2 households/ha, once again within the 1–2 households/ha that was the basis of the archaeological population estimates. This convergence of two separate and independent lines of evidence with the archaeological population estimates enhances confidence in them.

Estimated absolute populations for the Chifeng region, based on an area-density index as discussed above, also converge with other lines of evidence. In Chapter 2 Chifeng Site 342 was characterized on the basis of stratigraphic testing as having a sparse and patchy occupation in Warring States times; the corresponding population estimate (based on regional survey collections and the area-density index) was 35–70 people. The earlier Upper Xiajiadian occupation was—according to data from stratigraphic tests—both much more intensive and much more extensive, consistent with the population estimate of 550–1,100 based on the area-density index from regional survey. Stratigraphic tests suggested a still earlier Lower Xiajiadian occupation similar to that of Upper Xiajiadian times, and this was also consistent with the population of 600–1,200 estimated from the area-density index. The yet earlier Hongshan occupation seemed, on the basis of stratigraphic evidence, much smaller than any of the later occupations; it was estimated at 15–30 people from the area-density index. The area-density index suggested very tiny and ephemeral occupations in even earlier periods: 2–5 people in Zhaobaogou times and 8–15 in Xinglongwa times. These occupations were not revealed in stratigraphic testing at all. The area-density index, then, converts to population estimates that agree well with the results of stratigraphic testing for this site's occupation through more than 6,000 years from 6000 BC to 200 AD. At the Hongshan period village of Fushanzhuang in the Chifeng region, counting artifact concentrations representing individual household locations yielded a population estimate of 90–180, exactly the same as the estimate derived from the area-density index.

Mobility, Seasonality, Contemporaneity, and Interpretation

Population estimates based on both area and density of archaeological remains help us cope with some perennial complications of demographic analysis. One issue in particular is often thought of as three different problems: lack of contemporaneity of occupations whose archaeological remains we can record; seasonality of occupation in fundamentally sedentary populations; and highly mobile residence patterns. At base, these three really amount to a single issue: the fact that human groups have not stayed rooted in the same places from time immemorial. Human groups do move around the landscape and the only thing that differentiates these three problems of contemporaneity, seasonality, and high mobility is the temporal scale on which movement occurs. Groups we characterize as highly mobile move from one place to another several—or even many—times a year. Sedentary but seasonal groups change their location of residence a few times a year, often only twice; their pattern may be as simple as moving back and forth repeatedly between the same summer and winter locations.

What we label lack of contemporaneity of sites is also simply movement of groups from one location to another, but at much longer intervals. That is, living in one place for 50, 100, or 200 years and then moving to another place produces multiple sites. These appear to be contemporaneous sites if our only way to date them is to assign them all to the same 500-year period, but of course they are not truly contemporaneous. The often-voiced concern about these forms of movement is that it could be easy to count the same people several times in the different locations they occupy during a single archaeological period, thus inflating population estimates.

Combining area and density of archaeological remains as the basis for population estimates helps us deal with these issues effectively, as long as we conceptualize quite clearly just what population estimates based on both area and density really amount to. The starting point for combining area and density into population estimates was the thought that the amount of garbage deposited on the landscape is proportional to the number of people depositing garbage and the length of time they spend doing it (other things being equal, of course, and we have discussed some other such things and how they can in effect be equalized). The combination of area covered by archaeological remains with the density of those remains within the areas covered was proposed as a way of quantifying that garbage. As discussed in Chapter 2, the area-density index quantifies the garbage in terms of numbers of people and amounts of time—person-years of garbage. The "magic numbers" derived above for converting the area-density index into absolute numbers of people really convert the index into something slightly more complex combining both people and time—something like person-years of occupation.

Another way to think about it is that estimates of absolute populations based on areas and densities of ceramics pertaining to a particular period are estimates of the average population during that period. Thus, as noted before, an estimate of about 100 people in a particular locality for a particular period could mean that about 100 people lived there through the entire period, or that about 200 people lived there through half the period, or that 400 people lived there for one-fourth the period. All three come out to the same average population for the entire period. The absolute populations estimated from area and density, then, are not direct statements of the population at a particular moment in time, but of population averaged out over the length of a period.

This seems to introduce additional difficulty into the task of interpretation, and in some ways it does—although in other ways it simplifies things. Perhaps most important, it entirely eliminates the problem of double-counting people at non-contemporaneous sites to arrive at inflated regional totals. If 100 people (and their descendants) live in the same place through an entire period, an entire period's worth of garbage for 100 people is deposited there. If instead those 100 people live in one place for half the period, then move to another place and live there for the rest of the period, the same amount of garbage is deposited on the landscape, but half is in one place and half in another. If those 100 people live at four different places for one-fourth the length of the period each, the same amount of garbage is divided into fourths—one-fourth at each of four locations.

If combining area and density of artifacts gives a reasonable quantification of amounts of garbage, then the net total of area and density for the region will be the same in all three instances: a large area-density index for one place, or an area-density index half as large for each of two places, or an area-density index one-fourth as large for each of four places. This is true no matter what the temporal scale of the movement. The outcome is the same for 100 people who spend half the period in one place and half in another place, regardless of whether those halves mean the first half of the period and the second half of the period or the first half of each year and the second half of each year. A group that spends three months each year in each of four different places contributes exactly the same amount to an area-density index as a group the same size that moves four times during the entire period.

These equivalences assume that people's movements are contained within the region, or at least that to the extent people do leave the region on annual or longer cycles, others enter to replace them in similar average numbers. If, on the other hand, people only occupy a region during six winter months and abandon it entirely for someplace else for six summer months, the zero summer population means the momentary winter population is twice the estimated overall average population. An absolute population estimate based on area and density of remains is still an accurate account of the population, averaged over the entire length of the period.

As long as we interpret absolute population estimates based on area and density as long-term average population across the entire length of a period, then, some aspects of the issues of non-contemporaneity, seasonality, and high mobility are automatically dealt with. For some purposes, though, we need momentary population estimates—that is, the size of a group when it was in a place, not averaged together with zeros for the parts of the period when it was elsewhere. We can work toward this distinction when we can combine regional-scale totals with information (likely to come mostly from excavation of a sample of sites in the region) on duration of occupation, whether measured in centuries, years, months, weeks, or days. If data from several excavated sites indicate permanent year-round occupation of long duration, then the long-term average populations we estimate for local communities are not much different from momentary population estimates. And these are the conditions in which much regional settlement demographic analysis has been done. Residence is known to be year-round sedentary, and there is considerable continuity of occupation in particular locations through even more than just the length of a single period. These characteristics are sometimes taken for granted; it never hurts to be explicit about the evidence that backs up the assumptions.

Regions with ceramic sequences that discriminate only very long periods of time are especially at risk of obscuring finer-scale change by averaging rather different momentary populations across the long periods. One approach to this problem, of course, is to pursue ceramic analysis and chronometric dating to divide up the sequence into shorter periods. Success at such efforts, however, is simply not on the horizon for many regions, making it useful to think clearly about the meaning of the data we have now.

For Hongshan times in the Upper Daling valley in northeastern China, for example, multiple supra-local communities were delineated. The population of the largest was estimated from an area-density index at 500–1,000. Other evidence makes it unequivocal that this was a year-round sedentary population, but the period is 1,500 years long (4500–3000 BC), raising the very real possibility that this supra-local community's population may have varied substantially during Hongshan times. Although chronometric dates are not abundant, they do suggest that occupation in this supra-local community was spread through the full length of the period. Most likely it was founded by a population of modest size and grew to some population peak, which might have come at the end of the period or, alternatively, earlier in the period and been followed by population decline. If we wanted specifically to consider the maximum population size reached by this Hongshan regional polity when it was at its peak, we would have to consider the question of its pattern of growth. Whatever the exact sequence of change, the fact that more than just trivial populations are indicated throughout the period makes it unlikely that that the polity's population at its peak was much more than about twice the population average for the period. We could confidently say that this Hongshan regional polity's population never much exceeded 2,000 and might have been well below that at any given moment.

This conclusion may seem vague but it is an accurate characterization both of what we have found out and how precisely we know it. It is, moreover, a useful thing to say. The later Lower Xiajiadian period in northeastern China, for example, saw the development of many supra-local communities with populations, averaged across the entire period, that are estimated at 3,500–7,000. Since Lower Xiajiadian is a shorter period, momentary populations were probably closer to the estimated averages than for Hongshan times, but there were undoubtedly regional polities whose peak populations reached close to—or even exceeded—10,000. We are thus in position to say that the demographic scale of political integration at least doubled or tripled from Hongshan to Lower Xiajiadian times, from the very low thousands to around 10,000. Even very approximate estimates can be informative when the subject is change whose magnitude substantially exceeds the level of imprecision in the estimates.

Turning to a different temporal scale, seasonality data from several excavated sites might indicate that some occupations in a region were not year-round, but instead repeatedly occupied six-month winter camps. During the winter when they were actually occupied, then, those camps had roughly twice the estimated average population for their period. In a more complicated example, a Tunebo community in the Colombian Andes spends about 7 months each year in Cobaría at 1,300 m above sea level, 4 months in Sircurquesa at 1,000 m, and 1 month in Drabaría at 500 m. Ethnographic observation confirms the expectation that the amount of ceramics broken and discarded in each place is proportional to the amount of time spent there. Certain vessel forms occur in the highest proportions at Cobaría and in the lowest proportions at Drabaría. Judicious excavation of a few sites in such a situation could provide insight into this pattern, as well as a way of recognizing it in the proportions of different vessel forms in surface collections made from artifact scatters across a wide region.

The view is often expressed that the approaches to regional settlement demography discussed in this book are not valid for regions where mobility on some temporal scale is indicated. The situation is actually not nearly so bleak. Regional demographic data can be more fully and accurately interpreted when complemented with data from other sources, such as excavated sites and relevant ethnographic observations, that make it possible to document patterns of seasonality and mobility. This opportunity has not yet been explored as much as it should be in regional settlement demography, but the principles that make it possible to weave together regional-scale and site-scale data on mobility are clear.

APPROXIMATION, PRECISION, AND COMPARISON

In conclusion, archaeological estimates of absolute populations on a regional scale with a useful degree of precision are attainable. The subject must be approached cautiously and the archaeological results we have been able to achieve thus far are very approximate. For this reason we cringe when we read that someone estimates a population at 7,638. What this really means is something more like an estimate of 5,000–10,000. We cringe even more when we read that there was no demographic pressure on resources in a region because its prehistoric population was 7,638 and its carrying capacity was 8,765. It makes a world of difference to say that the region's population was 5,000–10,000 and it could support some 6,000–12,000 people ("carrying capacity" estimates are also very approximate, even aside from a series of much-discussed conceptual problems with the notion of carrying capacity). This latter, more realistic statement of such estimates leads to a different (and less definitive) conclusion: there might have been demographic pressure—perhaps even severe pressure—on resources, although it is not at all certain.

Unfortunately, the very approximate nature of the regional demographic estimates we can now make sometimes leaves our results inconclusive like this. This is not, however, always the case. It can turn out that we estimate population at 1,500–3,000 in a region whose local resources later easily supported, with the same subsistence technology, a population of 10,000–20,000. In a situation like this, scenarios of population pressure and intense competition over subsistence resources vanish like a puff of smoke for the earlier period because we have dared to make estimates of absolute population numbers and properly allowed for the fact that they are very approximate.

Absolute population estimates, as approximate as they are, provide a common currency for comparison of human communities in different regions. We regularly use terms like hamlet, village, and town to describe local communities that we take to provide rather different contexts for people's lives and their interactions with their neighbors. The properties we attribute to these different kinds of communities are varied, but they relate in many ways to their different demographic scales: towns, of course, are larger than villages, which in turn are larger than hamlets.

Using these concepts without attention to just what demographic scale is imagined for each can make comparisons between regions slippery. The Upper Xiajiadian period (1200–600 BC) in northeastern China has been described as a time when town dwelling, along with the social and economic patterns implied by towns, became solidly established. The Sintashta phenomenon (2100–1700 BC) of the southern Urals has been described as a "country of towns" that emerged rather suddenly and represented a new way of life, considered "proto-urban" by some. These two descriptions sound like they establish a commonality that could be the basis of interesting comparison. It is fundamental to any such comparison to recognize that Upper Xiajiadian town dwelling meant concentration of a large part of the population into local communities of around 10,000 inhabitants, with at least some reaching perhaps twice that size. Even the largest Sintashta towns, by contrast, had populations of probably less than 1,000 inhabitants;

some may have held as few as 100–200. It is quite clear when we make absolute population estimates concrete and explicit that whatever other similarities may or may not have been shared by the newly emerged larger Upper Xiajiadian and Sintashta local communities (and whatever labels we may attach to them), their demographic scale differed by more than an order of magnitude.

Local communities the size of the Sintashta towns had existed in northeastern China for at least 4,000 years prior to Upper Xiajiadian times. If the Sintashta towns appeared in the Basin of Mexico, their demographic scale would cause the larger ones to be labeled large, nucleated villages; and the smaller ones, small, nucleated villages. One of the most interesting questions to ask about the emergence of local communities that pull substantially larger numbers of people close together than before is how this larger demographic scale affects the possibilities for both cooperation and conflict. This cannot be done effectively without making absolute population estimates.

Archaeological estimates of absolute population numbers, then, are possible and worth the effort because they can tell us things we need to know. At the same time, we are the first to emphasize that the task is not for the faint of heart. The results are *very* approximate, almost always involve a certain amount of educated guessing, and there is need of constant effort to refine and improve our methods. But then what worthwhile archaeological conclusion is not subject to these same caveats?

SOME QUESTIONS AND ANSWERS

1. In the Valle de la Plata, shovel probes that were dug where vegetation cover was heavy provided a basis for arguing that artifact densities were uniformly low and that population estimates could be based on an average occupational density per hectare. What might have been done if the shovel probes had indicated substantial variation in artifact densities in different areas of occupation?

If the shovel probes from heavily vegetated areas indicated substantial variation in artifact density from place to place, the densities encountered in those same shovel probes might provide a basis for estimating the densities in areas where surface collection was possible but densities could not be reliably estimated. For example, suppose 200 shovel probes in occupations on level valley floors had densities averaging 8 sherds/m^2 with a standard deviation of 2 sherds/m^2, and that 300 shovel probes in upland locations yielded an average of 2 sherds/m^2 with a standard deviation of 4 sherds/m^2. This amounts to a sampling estimate for valley floor occupations of 8 ± 0.28 sherds/m^2 and for upland locations of 2 ± 0.45 sherds/m^2, both at the 95% confidence level. Such small error ranges would give us high confidence in assigning a density of 8 sherds/m² to valley floor occupations and 2 sherds/m² to upland occupations where surface densities could not actually be measured well. We would then have areas and estimated densities on which to base an area-density index and thus absolute population estimates.

The process of estimating densities on the basis of the shovel probes could involve more variables and more complicated statistics, but the approach would follow the same fundamental logic. Although working with absolute population estimates may bring this issue of variation in artifact density to our attention, it is embedded in any form of using area and density together as a population proxy. This question, then, is just as much a question for Chapter 2 as for Chapter 4. Estimates of densities for places where they cannot be measured (based on shovel probes in different locations) would be applied in the initial calculation of an area-density index, and would thus make analyses depending only on that population proxy—as well as absolute population estimates—more accurate.

2. In some regions surface conditions make it possible to assess artifact densities in some locations, but not in others. You suspect that some settlements contain much denser remains than others but your permit for archaeological research does not allow the excavation of shovel probes. Can absolute population estimates be made?

This is a potential problem, not just for absolute population estimates but for relative ones as well. Area by itself seems a less reliable population proxy than area combined with density, but area by itself may simply be the best one can do for regional-scale demographic analysis in this situation. To convert this proxy into an absolute estimate, information on excavated sites or census data may provide an average number of inhabitants per occupied hectare. Any batch of numbers, after all, does have an average; it's just that this one may come with a larger standard error, meaning that estimates of absolute population based on it are even more approximate than usual, and should be stated with an even wider gap between minimum and maximum estimates.

3. The questions at the end of Chapter 2 suggested that the volumes of Near Eastern tells might be used as a population proxy similar to an area-density index. Could estimates of absolute population numbers be based on volumes of tells?

Precisely this has in fact been suggested. The proposed logic is that, since most of the volume of a tell consists of the collapsed remains of mudbrick residential architecture, the key to absolute population estimates is determining the average volume of mud brick in a single-family residence. Extensively excavated tells provide numerous architectural plans and preservation is sometimes such that wall heights can be estimated. Very similar houses, moreover, are still built in some areas today. This information could provide the basis for estimating the mean volume of mud brick in a family's residence, and since there are plans for different periods, the volume could be adjusted to changes in house size through time. The calculated volume of tell deposit dating to a particular period could be divided by the average for that period to estimate the number of families, and a constant minimum and maximum number of family members could be used to convert that into a population estimate. If house plans suggested changes in family size through time, the minimum and maximum family sizes could be adjusted as well.

4. For regional settlement demography, one hopes to use a ceramic classification scheme that relies heavily on paste, temper, surface finish, and other characteristics observable even on small body sherds (as discussed in Chapter 2). It still may happen that collections from some sites are so badly eroded that many cannot be identified. If the unidentified sherds are not counted into the densities for their respective periods, those densities will be unrealistically low, depressing the population estimates for those particular sites. Can anything be done to compensate for this?

Sometimes the overall sherd density value for a location (including unidentified sherds) has been divided between periods according to the proportions of identified sherds. For example, a systematic collection in 10 m² (see Chapter 5) might yield 6 sherds from period A, 14 sherds from period B, and 16 unidentified sherds. The overall density would be a total of 36 sherds in 10 m², so 3.60 sherds/m². Since 30% of the 20 identified sherds were from period A and 70% from period B, 30% of the overall density (or 1.08 sherds/m²) would be assigned to period A and 70% (or 2.52 sherds/m²) to period B. This would avoid deflating the overall density from 3.60 sherds/m² to 2.00 sherds/m² by counting only identified sherds, and would yield population estimates for both periods that are more likely to be more accurate in comparison with other locations in the region. Since the large number of unidentified sherds in this case is due to the effects of erosion, it seems likely to affect all periods similarly, giving us confidence in proceeding in this way. Finally, the results might not be too different from those based only on identified sherds, or the difference might be substantial.

It is easy enough to simply follow this approach to apportioning overall sherd densities throughout the analysis of a region, and guard against the possibly uneven effects of erosion at different sites. It would disturb this logic, however, if some periods had high proportions of well-fired, hard sherds highly resistant to erosion. If that were the case, this way of apportioning the overall densities could go astray unless the differing effects of erosion on the sherds of different periods could be compensated for in the calculations. Just as with Question #3, making absolute population estimates calls this issue especially to our attention, but it too is just as much an issue for Chapter 2, since it involves not just assigning absolute numbers but how best to calculate densities in the first place.

5. We may suspect that elites have more possessions, including pottery, than other people do; they may also host special activities, such as feasting, which we think of as producing large amounts of garbage. Can these factors be assessed and compensated for in making absolute population estimates?

In most cases these factors do not need to be assessed and compensated for in making absolute population estimates. They are, for example, already automatically accounted for in the process of establishing the relationship between an area-density index and an absolute population estimate. If this relationship is based largely on excavated sites, the local communities those sites represent presumably contain the same average range of activities and elites as the local communities documented at the regional scale and for which the area-density index has been calculated.

The average amount of garbage deposited on the landscape per person is an average across an entire population, elite and non-elite, and includes the garbage produced in the full range of activities common to residential locations—including feasting and other special activities. The intensity of such activities will of course vary from place to place, and the quantity of garbage produced will vary from household to household for myriad reasons. The average, however, is the average across all of this. The gap between the minimum and maximum estimates is an expression of the variation we know exists around this average, so factors like elite pottery use, feasting, and the like are already allowed for.

SUGGESTED READINGS

"Floor Area and Settlement Population" by Raoul Naroll (*American Antiquity* 27:587–589, 1962). Analyzes the relationship between house floor area and number of residents across various cultures and arrives at an average of 10 m^2 of roofed area per person.

"Population Estimation from Floor Area: A Restudy of 'Naroll's Constant'" by Barton McCaul Brown (*Cross-Cultural Research* 21:1–49, 1987). Takes up again the issue from Naroll's paper, recognizes a large number of complicating factors, and arrives at an average of 6 m^2 per person. Although both Naroll and Brown were both quite tentative about the reliability of their conclusions, these averages have been used a good bit in estimating populations.

Precolumbian Population History in the Maya Lowlands edited by T. Patrick Culbert and Don S. Rice (University of New Mexico Press, Albuquerque, 1990). A collection of papers by different authors considering populations, population change, and methods of estimating absolute populations at different scales in the lowland Maya area.

"Explaining the Neolithic Demographic Transition" by Jean-Pierre Bocquet-Appel, in *The Neolithic Demographic Transition and Its Consequences* edited by Jean-Pierre Bocquet-Appel and Ofer Bar-Yosef (Springer-Verlag, New York, pp. 35–55, 2008). Explores the relationship between population growth and changes in family size.

"Structure Abandonment in Villages" by Catherine M. Cameron (*Archaeological Method and Theory* 3:155–194, 1991). A cross-cultural examination of the factors involved in the abandonment of house structures and thus of the lengths of their useful lives.

Emergent Complexity on the Mongolian Steppe: Mobility, Territoriality, and the Development of Early Nomadic Polities by Jean-Luc Houle (unpublished Ph.D. dissertation, University of Pittsburgh, 2010). Direct connections between ethnographic observations and the Bronze Age archaeological record for estimating populations with an area-density index in a context of substantial seasonal mobility on an annual scale. Relates to the field methods discussed in Chapter 5 as well.

"Settlement Pattern Survey in the Rizhao Area: A Preliminary Effort to Consider Han and Pre-Han Demography" by Fang Hui, Gary M. Feinman, Anne P. Underhill, and Linda M. Nicholas (*Bulletin of the Indo-Pacific Prehistory Association* 24:79–82, 2004). The details of one of the examples used in this chapter for basing archaeological population estimates on links to modern census data and then using Han Dynasty census data as an ex post facto check.

"A Test of the Relationship Between Site Size and Population" by Katharina J. Schreiber and Keith W. Kintigh (*American Antiquity* 61:573–579, 1996). Archaeological data and Spanish Colonial census data for the Carhuarazo Valley demonstrate that the relationship between area and absolute population is complicated but tractable, especially if some additional variables are taken into account.

Prehispanic Change in the Mesitas Community: Documenting the Development of a Chiefdom's Central Place in San Agustín, Huila, Colombia by Victor González Fernández (University of Pittsburgh Memoirs in Latin American Archaeology, No. 18, 2007). Identification of individual household locations in a very dispersed community by following up regional-scale settlement survey with closely spaced shovel probes. Provides one of the examples discussed above of direct connection of archaeologically based population estimates with regional-scale area and density information. Shovel probes are also part of the consideration of field methods in Chapter 5.

CHAPTER 5

HOW CAN WE COLLECT REGIONAL SETTLEMENT DATA FOR DEMOGRAPHIC ANALYSIS?

The fieldwork upon which regional settlement demography is based is usually referred to as regional archaeological survey. Archaeological survey is a staple in books on field methods in archaeology and several books are dedicated entirely to the methods of archaeological survey. It is generally recognized that different regions present archaeological records with different characteristics and that methods of survey, like methods of excavation, need to be adjusted to the conditions in which they are used.

A more important point is that methods of survey (again like methods of excavation) need to be adjusted to the research questions they aim to answer, and some approaches to regional survey do not lead to a sound population proxy. This obviously means that absolute population estimates cannot be made, but it also means that the kinds of analysis discussed in Chapter 3 are on very shaky ground as well, since these analyses assume that the numbers analyzed are proportional to population. If it is not possible to justify the assumption that number of sites or area of sites is proportional to population, then it will not do to carry out analyses like those described in Chapter 3—pretending that they are just analyses of sites or areas and that the difficulties of archaeological demography or the problems of inappropriate field methods have been avoided.

FINDING SITES TO DIG

The two most common purposes for regional survey in archaeology have long been, and probably continue to be, locating promising sites to dig and inventorying archaeological resources for cultural heritage management. Both, of course, are worthy aims, but surveys carried out for either of these purposes may not be of much use for demographic analysis—not that this necessarily prevents the publication of some very unsound conclusions of a fundamentally demographic nature based on such surveys.

As an example, the first survey of the Tonosí region in central Panama was carried out around 1970 to locate sites where excavation could recover good samples of ceramics for a study of ceramic styles and their origins. Some 500 km² were explored; a number of sites were located; stratigraphic tests were made at a good many of these and a few were excavated more extensively. Analysis of the burials and their grave goods eventually revealed a good bit about social organization in the region, and the published results include maps locating the sites that were identified for each phase. The number of sites was used as a population proxy to make statements about the distribution of population across the region and demographic growth through time.

Not at all surprisingly, a more intensive survey of 50 km² of this area—carried out 40 years later to collect data for demographic analysis—found considerably more evidence of pre-Hispanic occupation than just the sites on the earlier maps. Based on area and density of remains, the earliest occupation in the 50 km² area (El Indio, 200–500 AD) consisted of about 400 inhabitants. This increased dramatically to about 2,500 in La Cañaza times (500–1000 AD) and then modestly again to around 3,700 for the Bijaguales phase (1000–1522 AD). The 1970 survey recorded no El Indio sites, one La Cañaza site, and four Bijaguales sites in this area, giving a very different impression of population change through time—especially making growth from La Cañaza to Bijaguales times seem much more dramatic than it evidently was. Several issues converge to produce this outcome. Because the 1970 survey was intended largely to identify sites for excavation, it was less systematic and complete and at a much lower level of resolution; and number of sites is a poor population proxy (see Chapter 2). These issues would create a lot of random noise that would interfere with demographic analysis.

A more important issue, however, is sampling bias in the 1970 survey. The five sites it recorded in the 50 km² surveyed more intensively later on were all sites with unusually high densities of materials, and three of them had mounds visible on the surface. It makes perfectly good sense for a survey aimed at locating sites where excavations would yield abundant elaborate ceramics to focus attention on high-density sites or sites with mounds. The problem this creates for demographic analysis, however, is that it systematically underrepresents the sites of lower density without mounds where the vast majority of the population lived in all periods. In the Tonosí region, not atypically, this bias toward dense sites or sites with mounds correlates with time. High-density sites are especially rare in El Indio times, become more common in La Cañaza times, and increase even more in frequency in Bijaguales times. Mounds occur only in the Bijaguales phase. In addition to the largely random noise from being less intensive or complete, and of lower resolution, then, the 1970 survey introduces a systematic bias in favor of finding La Cañaza evidence and a much stronger bias in favor of Bijaguales.

Sampling bias of various kinds is a persistent problem when surveys carried out to find good sites for excavation are used as the basis for demographic conclusions. This problem can lead to truly extreme outcomes. The Alto Magdalena of Colombia has long been known for its monumental pre-Hispanic tombs and statues. There was a time when it was pronounced to be a zone without human occupation, a sacred region to which people came from distant places to bury their distinguished dead. To be sure, no one who said this thought of it as prehistoric demography, but it's a statement about how many people lived in the Alto Magdalena. It turns out that well over 10% of the surface area of the Alto Magdalena, and over 20% in some sectors, has evidence of pre-Hispanic occupation—by worldwide standards an extraordinarily large proportion of the landscape to show evidence of ancient occupation—but these fairly unimpressive sherd scatters were simply not considered "sites" and escaped notice entirely, because attention was so strongly focused on the excavation of monumental remains.

In much the same way, Hongshan period sites in northeastern China are still considered by some to be rigidly divided between habitation sites on the one hand and ceremonial sites on the other, with their remains of stone-faced platforms and tombs. The ceremonial sites are sometimes generically described as not associated with zones of occupation and distant from them, despite the fact that systematic survey in the Chifeng, Upper Daling, and Niuheliang regions unequivocally demonstrates associated living areas and that many sites with ceremonial architecture are at the core of residential communities. Hongshan period habitation sites, like those in the Alto Magdalena, are very often unprepossessing sherd scatters that easily escape notice when attention is heavily focused on public architecture. Residential structures and features are often poorly preserved and there is little to excavate at most of the sherd (and burned daub) scatters that document habitation.

In both the Alto Magdalena and northeastern China, surveys very strongly biased toward recording sites that are promising for the excavation of large-scale architecture have been used to make erroneous conclusions about where people did and did not live.

LARGE-SCALE CULTURAL HERITAGE INVENTORIES

Large-scale inventories of sites for heritage protection purposes have sometimes been explicitly argued to be in a different category, one that is more useful for demographic analysis. The case has recently been made for using

An Atlas of Chinese Cultural Relics in this way, explicitly taking the number of sites in different periods and regions across northern China as a population proxy to monitor large-scale patterns of population growth, decline, and movement. This national survey is certainly among the largest scale, most comprehensive, and most systematic of all such cultural heritage inventories; when complete in published form it will consist of 32 volumes, most of which are actually two thick books. Demographic analysis was not included among the objectives of the survey, but if any national heritage inventory is able to sustain demographic analysis, this may well be it.

Systematic smaller-scale surveys of the Chifeng and Upper Daling regions in northern China, carried out with methodologies designed specifically to collect data for demographic analysis, provide a vantage point from which to consider the issue. The Chifeng region is covered in the Inner Mongolia Autonomous Region volume of the atlas; the Upper Daling region, in the Liaoning Province volume. The national atlas dates sites of the relevant time frame only as Neolithic or Bronze Age; the same time span was divided into six periods in the regional surveys. Obviously there are considerable advantages to greater chronological precision, but this is not a fatal flaw in using the national survey for demographic analysis—even the six-period scheme consists of very long periods. For comparison with the national survey, the results from Chifeng and Upper Daling can be collapsed into the two longer periods.

For the Chifeng region, the national survey counts 8 Neolithic and 81 Bronze Age sites (in 1,234 km^2); for Upper Daling, 15 Neolithic and 26 Bronze Age sites (in 200 km^2). Numbers of sites in the national survey, then, would indicate that the Upper Daling region had a Neolithic population density more than 10 times greater than Chifeng's (7.5 sites/100 km^2 vs. 0.6 sites/100 km^2). Systematic survey for demographic analysis does reveal a denser population in the Upper Daling region, but only about twice as dense as Chifeng's. For the Bronze Age, Upper Daling's population density was about 25% lower than Chifeng's, rather than 100% higher as indicated by the number of sites recorded in the national survey.

Looked at another way, both the national survey and systematic assessment of area and density of remains indicate Bronze Age population growth for both regions, but the rates estimated are wildly different. For the national survey, Chifeng's population increase was tenfold, compared with a 24-fold increase from area and density of remains. In Upper Daling the national survey puts population increase at less than twofold, but area and density indicate nearly a ninefold increase. Even by the standards of approximation we have insisted on for demographic estimates, these are starkly divergent pictures—ones that would lead to very different broad conclusions about human populations.

In addition to the issues of random noise and low resolution, efforts to use the national survey for demographic analysis must rely on the poor population proxy of number of sites. Most important, though, at least two sources of systematic bias seem to affect the figures from the national survey. First, the Upper Daling region contains a well-known excavated Neolithic Hongshan ceremonial site (Dongshanzui) and cultural heritage officials are admirably attuned to Hongshan period remains. Consequently, Hongshan remains are especially well documented for Upper Daling, skewing the comparison based on the national survey strongly toward Upper Daling for Neolithic times. Second, Bronze Age remains of both Lower and Upper Xiajiadian periods are abundant and impressive in Chifeng, including surface remains of stone-built residential architecture, burials, and occasionally spectacular fortifications. This multitude of obviously large and important sites depresses the relative apparent value of the much more numerous sherd scatters, which come to seem hardly worth recording as part of a heritage inventory. The Bronze Age population is thus particularly underrated in Chifeng, compounding the effect of especially effective registration of Neolithic sites in Upper Daling.

These discrepancies are, again, not just a consequence of random noise and the naturally lower resolution of a vastly larger-scale survey. They are the result of complicated (and strong) biases about what to record and what not to record, biases that vary considerably from region to region and period to period. They will not somehow just average out to a reasonably accurate larger-scale picture of population; these biases will persist and skew the resulting impressions of population change through time, as well as distribution through space. Even aside from this problem—severe as it is—it is doubtful that we could learn much about the evolving nature of human communities, their social or political organization, or their environmental adaptations and subsistence or economic systems from a demographic average across hundreds of thousands of square kilometers. The processes that produce change in these phenomena operate at smaller regional and local scales that would be systematically washed out of such a coarse-grained view, even if it were an accurate one.

To be clear, surveys capable of sustaining demographic analysis can certainly be carried out in a project-specific resource management context. In this section we refer to extensive ongoing programs to inventory the archaeological sites of an entire province or nation, especially focused on the sites most worth attempting to protect from destruction by development. Such inventories are vital to the preservation of the archaeological record. Their results, however, do not provide an adequate foundation for any kind of demographic conclusions.

SURVEY DATA FOR DEMOGRAPHY

It is useful to think about why sound demographic information does not come from surveys aimed at finding sites to dig or producing large-scale cultural heritage inventories; it helps make clear how to collect better data for demographic analysis.

Appropriate survey methodology for regional demographic analysis has more than a little in common with census taking. Adjectives like *complete*, *comprehensive*, *systematic*, *consistent*, and *unbiased* have fairly clear meanings in the context of population censuses. To be useful, a census of population must be complete and comprehensive. That is, it must count everyone; just going to some chosen places scattered through the region to be censused and counting the people at those places will not do. The census must be systematic and consistent about counting people in the same way throughout. For example, a decision must be made about whether to count students and soldiers in their dormitories and barracks or at the addresses where their families live. If some census takers do it one way and some the other, the quality of the data will be damaged. It probably could be done either way, but it must be done consistently.

Most complicated, the census must be unbiased. Sampling biases can occur in many different, and often insidious, ways. Sometimes when the census taker knocks, no one is at home. If these families just go uncounted, obviously the final number is an undercount, so the census taker must return later—perhaps again and again, although it must all stop somewhere and some people will remain forever uncounted. If the census taker only works during normal business hours, it is likely that many working homeowners will never answer the door and a serious bias against people who work will have been introduced. This has worse impacts than just undercounting, since it will also systematically reduce the numbers for things like employment rates or income levels that are based on census data.

Likewise, a regional archaeological survey that aims to provide data for demographic analysis must be complete and comprehensive. Just finding some sites in a region, even if they're the most important ones by some criterion, won't do. The entire regional landscape must be examined for archaeological evidence. We must know that blank areas on the maps we produce are not blank just because the archaeologists never got there; we must be able to confidently take that blankness to mean a documented absence of archaeological remains. Examination of the region must be systematic and consistent. There are many choices about just how to examine the landscape (see below); once made, these decisions must be carried out in the same way throughout the region. It won't do to diminish the intensity of survey coverage at the western extreme of the region so as to go faster late in the season, because that part was left for last and too much time was lost to rain days. Sampling bias is a multifaceted subject but making survey coverage complete, comprehensive, systematic, and consistent takes us a long way toward avoiding bias. The remainder of this chapter considers a number of issues of field methods related to these thoughts.

DELIMITING A REGION

Perhaps the first step in deciding where to survey is to ask "How big should a region be?" When asked how long a man's legs should be, Abraham Lincoln is reputed to have answered that they should be long enough to reach the ground. Along similar lines, for purposes of demographic analysis a region should be big enough to include the demographic phenomenon to be studied, although we may not really know what this is until after we study it.

A region as small as a few square kilometers can encompass a local community, but it is not large enough to permit observation of that community's neighbors, or to pursue the possibility of supra-local groupings that may comprise essential social, political, or economic units in sedentary complex societies. Small polities, at least, can often be surveyed in their entirety; indeed, it is often possible to survey a number of neighboring small chiefly polities and delineate their limits and other demographic parameters with some care. Large states may substantially exceed the areas that can be surveyed by the methods discussed in this book. Demographically much smaller groups of mobile hunter-gatherers or herders may also be spread through substantially larger areas than can be surveyed by these methods. National heritage inventories do not provide a reliable way to look at the demographics of such large regions (see above), but multiple regional surveys of, say, a few hundred square kilometers each—in different parts of an extensive polity—can give us insight into the relations between the parts in such an overarching organization.

Criteria for drawing the boundaries of a study region often bring together environmental features and the demographic patterns related to supra-local communities. These latter, of course, emerge from the survey itself, but regional survey projects are often multi-year efforts, so it is possible for these emerging patterns to inform decisions about how to expand and delimit a survey region as the work progresses—at least if analysis and interpretation keep pace with fieldwork instead of being postponed until the end.

Examples of Regions

In the Basin of Mexico, environmental features were important in the a priori definition of an area to survey. The region is (or was) an internally drained basin of some 7,000 km^2 with a system of lakes and swamps in its center, surrounded concentrically by a fertile level lakeshore plain, then by a sloping piedmont zone, and eventually around most of its perimeter by high mountains with steep slopes. These mountain barriers could easily be guessed to delimit a region that had meaning not only in environmental terms, but also in social, political, and demographic terms—although this did not imply any assumption that social or political entities would necessarily correspond to these limits. Indeed, demographic data from the survey helped make it possible to see that early in the sequence of sedentary human occupation, the Basin of Mexico contained multiple independent small polities; that political unification came later; and that this was eventually followed by the extension of political domination from capitals located in the Basin to a much larger surrounding territory. Since the central lake and modern Mexico City occupy a substantial part of the region, the area actually surveyed in two big blocks finally totaled about 2,500 km^2 (see Figure 1.1).

The Alto Magdalena is an extensive, sharply dissected, and environmentally heterogeneous zone along the eastern slopes of the central Andean *cordillera* in Colombia. The monumental tombs and statues that attracted attention to its apparently complex pre-Hispanic societies occur at a large number of sites scattered through some 3,500 km^2. Human occupation is sharply limited by high elevation toward the northwest, but in other directions there are no such obviously meaningful environmental limits. Regional survey was first carried out in what came to be called the western zone of the Valle de la Plata (see Figure 1.1), an area of 317 km^2 of steep, well-watered slopes at 1200–2400 m above sea level that revealed surprisingly high population density and small regional polities covering some 100–150 km^2 each. Subsequent survey of the eastern zone of the Valle de la Plata, totaling 169 km^2 at lower elevations in drier, flatter river valley floors, revealed very low populations taking little part in the consolidation of small regional polities that had occurred on the higher slopes. The central zone of the Valle de la Plata consisted of 73 km^2 that documented a sharp transition between the higher demographic densities to the west and the lower ones to the east—a transition that corresponded quite clearly to a sharp change in environmental conditions.

Finally, a zone of 323 km^2 to the southwest was surveyed. This included the highest density of monumental tombs and statues and the sites with the largest collections of such remains. Supra-local communities probably comprising small regional polities strongly resembled those of the western zone in the Valle de la Plata. In this instance, then, overall patterns through an area of 3,500 km^2 were documented by surveying a total of 882 km^2 in four separate patches. This strategy was able to succeed in part because the pattern of supra-local organization consisted of relatively small repetitive units, and the final delineation of survey boundaries relied on both environmental parameters and the demographic patterns emerging from the research.

In the Rizhao region of Shandong Province in eastern China, the Longshan period (2600–1900 BC) walled town of Liangchengzhen was the central focus of a region initially delimited with the hope of including much or all of the hinterland of this early central place and presumed capital of a regional polity (see Figure 1.1). The survey was subsequently expanded southward to encompass some 1,120 km^2 and the walled capital of a neighboring regional polity, as well as much of its hinterland (and the area was later expanded even farther). The area did include two river drainages, but the patterning emerging from ongoing analysis of the survey results played an even more central role in determining the survey limits than in either the Basin of Mexico or the Alto Magdalena.

Surveys carried out by dozens of projects through some 40 years of loosely collaborative research in the state of Oaxaca, Mexico, have covered some 10,000 km^2 by methods like those described in this book. Each project was approached as a regional settlement study in its own terms, but the cumulative result is a rich and detailed picture of what has been labeled a macroregion, within which regional trajectories of complex society development followed divergent but intertwined paths. Creating a macroregional synthesis by combining regional-scale surveys that collected appropriate data for demographic reconstruction is a convincing and productive way to enlarge the scale of analysis, and capture the relationships and variation among the different parts of a macroregion, that are essential to understanding the dynamics of social, political, and economic change.

Much smaller survey zones (100 km^2 or less) have often provided invaluable documentation of a single small, independent, supra-local chiefly community. A city-state might also be encompassed in a region of this size. For many prehistoric states, 100 km^2 around the capital would encompass only a very small central core of the full polity. In the lands around the Mediterranean, regional survey can refer to zones of only a few square kilometers around a major settlement. Research at this scale can be extremely important and enlightening, and it is a large enough scale that data are likely to need to be collected from the surface by methods related to those discussed in this chapter. The scale of demographic analysis we have in mind in writing this book, however, is larger, and when archaeologists working in most parts of the world say "region," they usually refer to at least several tens of square kilometers—if not hundreds or thousands.

Carrying Out a Survey

Within the boundaries of the survey area, teams of three or so surveyors walk systematically back and forth across the entire landscape in a pattern of rough transects at a fixed interval. Unsystematic visits to assorted localities thought likely to have sites will not do, because this will inevitably introduce substantial sampling bias into the data. The interval between surveyors' transects varies substantially in different projects. Obviously, if the interval between surveyors is 50 m, then surface scatters smaller than 50 m across will often escape detection. Even though regional surveys are often described as "complete coverage," they all have a discovery threshold below which surface scatters will often go undetected—either because the scatters are small enough to lie between transects, or because they are so sparse that a surveyor could walk right across them without seeing an artifact. There is always a trade-off between intensity and area of coverage. Larger intervals between pedestrian transects mean missing more small, sparse artifact scatters, but make it possible to survey a larger region. Setting the balance depends on the region, its archaeological record, and the research questions that drive the survey.

In very flat regions, survey transects are sometimes laid out on a rigid grid and surveyors follow them by GPS. In most regions topography makes this practice impossible, and "transects" are much more uneven and opportunistic than the word implies. The interval to the next surveyor's transect is judged by eye. Even in flat regions, surveyors not tied to straight GPS tracks can veer this way and that to try to spot artifacts where surface visibility is especially good and to make other relevant observations. The most efficient and productive surveyors focus their attention not on their GPS screens, but on the landscape and whatever it offers in the way of evidence of ancient human activities.

It goes without saying that maps of survey results need to show the boundaries of the survey area so that readers will know just what area was subjected to systematic inspection, and which are the areas that are devoid of sites because they are beyond the limits of the study. Or, well, perhaps it doesn't go without saying, since a number of survey reports in our libraries lack precisely this information.

MEASURING OCCUPIED AREA IN THE FIELD

Area of occupation is the measurement most fundamental to good population proxies in many world regions where rooms and structures, for example, cannot be counted on a regional scale. In the field in areas of good surface visibility, this usually means measuring the areas of surface artifact scatters. And since the size of the occupation might well change from one period to another during the span of occupation in the locality, the areas of surface scatter would need to be measured separately for the artifacts of each period present. The areas of surface scatters have been measured and recorded in a number of different ways. We will consider several of these, in turn, using the example artifact scatter in Figure 5.1. To simplify, the discussion will be mostly synchronic, but the measurements discussed must be made separately for artifacts of each period.

Site Sizes versus Mapping Individual Artifacts

If the scatter in Figure 5.1 were surrounded by a large zone without artifacts, it would approximate a clearly defined single-component archaeological site as traditionally imagined. Once the scatter in Figure 5.1 is discovered and thought of as a site, its area might well be measured as anything from about 0.25 ha to 1.7 ha to 3.4 ha, since its limits might well be approximated as indicated by any of the three ellipses in the figure. Different surveys have applied different standards of just how dense the artifacts must be to qualify a scatter as a site, and when the density falls below the level taken to be important, the site is considered to have ended. It is extremely rare for reports of survey results to be specific about what this density is. It is not often considered explicitly in the field either, since the workers in a given survey are likely to share a rough, implicit, a priori notion of what constitutes a "real" site and what is only a few artifacts in a field and not to be recorded.

Often the measurement of the area of a site is a very quick thing, based on walking around a bit and then estimating that the site is a rough ellipse around 60 m long and 50 m wide (like the smaller ellipse in Figure 5.1). How large those numbers are depends on how far archaeologists walked in several directions, the exact paths they took, and their implicit notion of

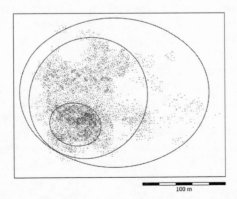

Figure 5.1. An artifact scatter based on an actual distribution of Hongshan period artifacts in the Upper Daling region. The size of this site might well be estimated as any of the three ellipses, following procedures used by different surveys.

how low artifact density had to get before they stopped and said, "It ends here." Such measurements of site area are better than nothing but they don't represent best practices. Most often survey carried out in this mode pays little attention to the different areas covered by materials of different periods. The lack of this latter information seriously degrades the usefulness of area as a population proxy except in those rare regions where sites are mostly single component. Estimating site area separately for each period in this mode of survey is obviously an even rougher approximation. And finally, a map with archaeological sites as point locations for which estimated areas have been written down is not suitable for some kinds of analysis, since the relationships between the edges of the actual polygons covered by artifacts can matter.

At the opposite methodological extreme are approaches sometimes labeled siteless survey, in which each individual artifact is mapped in place. This approach is only viable for very tiny areas, compared with the scale of analysis dealt with in this book. Even if resources were available to map all individual artifacts in an area of tens, hundreds, or thousands of square kilometers, it would not be a wise use of those resources.

Areas by Collection Unit Polygons

Much more efficient methods of recording data on artifact distribution across areas of this size have been developed that provide an appropriate level of resolution. One of these is to conceive of the survey area as composed of a very large number of small spatial units, not unlike the way excavation methodology usually starts with the imposition of a grid of squares on the area to be excavated. Often called collection units, these do not necessarily comprise a rectilinear grid of perfect squares, but are polygons adjusted to landscape features (that in many cases are eventually seen to correspond well to the boundaries of artifact scatters). Typically a maximum size is set for these units, which is also an expression of the spatial resolution of the survey.

Survey crews walking systematically back and forth across the landscape along approximate transects envision their paths as going through and inspecting a series of such spatial units. The collection units are mentally crossed off, one after another, as not having surface artifacts. When surface artifacts are spotted, survey teams reorganize to delineate the boundaries of collection units more formally and to collect artifacts separately in each unit (by methods discussed more fully in the next section). If an entire artifact scatter is smaller than the maximum collection unit size, the boundary of the artifact scatter simply becomes the boundary of a single collection unit (which is thus smaller than the maximum size) and a single artifact collection is made to represent that unit. If the artifact scatter is larger than the maximum collection unit size, then the scatter is divided into several collection units—whose boundaries are formally delineated—and each unit is represented by its own separate artifact collection.

Most archaeologists who have surveyed with such an approach have found it efficient to print aerial photographs or satellite imagery on paper for survey teams to use as maps in the field. Territory is crossed off on these maps as it is examined and found to be without artifacts, maintaining a continual record of the progress of examining the landscape and helping to ensure that different teams do not leave gaps between their coverage or waste time surveying the same territory twice. The spatial limits of collection units are drawn on these maps as well—along with their identifying numbers—using landscape features to locate them, with assistance from GPS units as necessary (Figure 5.2).

In regions with large expanses of featureless landscape, it may be necessary to actually walk around the limits of collection units and record GPS tracks, but this slows down the fieldwork considerably—even allowing for the fact that collection unit boundaries can then be downloaded instead of digitized from paper maps. Digitizing goes very fast with good software (although this is not, unfortunately, an accurate description of the digitizing tools included in some of the most-used GIS software). It would take well over an hour of a survey team's time just to walk the 9.3 km required to record the collection unit polygons in Figure 5.2 as GPS tracks; they could all be digitized in less than 10 minutes of one person's time. The publishers of the Yellow Pages got it right long ago: let your fingers do the walking. As of this writing, the hardware and software exist to make this work all digital in the field—with tablets compact enough to carry easily but large enough to present a zoomable satellite image at a useful size, integrated with the GPS location technology of the tablet, and with the possibility of drawing collection unit boundaries and assigning them numbers directly on a touch screen.

This approach to survey methodology is a direct outgrowth of methods first developed in the Basin of Mexico. It continued to develop as variants of it were used in many regional surveys in Mesoamerica, subsequently in South America, and more recently in scattered parts of the Old World. The widespread availability of high-quality georectified satellite imagery has been a major boon. Quite a number of projects using fundamentally this methodology do not formalize the definition of collection units quite so much or even use the term "collection unit," speaking instead (for example) of "field by field" survey. Some of these surveys, especially where archaeological remains are strongly clustered on the landscape, call what they find "sites," a term we have not used in our description of this form of survey.

The lack of fully standardized terminology and the presence of much variation in field methods can sometimes make it a challenge to know just how similar are the field methodologies of different survey projects, even

Figure 5.2. A satellite image used in the field to record survey progress and collection unit limits with their numbers. This image covers 1 km east-to-west, and was printed on letter-size paper for a scale of 1:5,000. A grid with UTM coordinates provides a link to GPS location, and a box 50 by 50 m in the top center reminds survey teams of how large a collection unit of 0.25 ha appears at this scale. Sites as traditionally imagined are clearly visible here; some are small (less than the 0.25 ha maximum area of collection units), but larger ones are subdivided into separate collection units.

when methods are fully described (which is often not the case). At some level no two are truly just alike, but we have described in what we hope are clear—though not universally used—terms the central conceptual elements of a broad family of survey methodologies widely employed for recovering data able to sustain a range of fundamentally demographic analyses.

Contiguous areas sometimes substantially exceeding 1,000 km² have been surveyed in this way with collection units of 1 ha or less. Survey teams might walk transects spaced 30–50 m apart, meaning that two or three surveyors cross each potential collection unit. Sometimes spacing is wider. Of course the speed of coverage varies in different regions depending on topography, vegetation, how much material is being discovered and collected, how close vehicles can deliver survey teams to the tracts where they are working, and all the other familiar foibles of fieldwork. In many instances a survey team of three can cover around 1 km² in a day's work. Where this rate is possible, a group of 12 fieldworkers could survey 1,000 km² in three field seasons, each three months long. A regional survey on this scale is thus not necessarily a megaproject if the work is efficiently organized. If there are many small- or low-density artifact scatters that might be missed using larger intervals, collection units can be 0.25 ha (50 by 50 m) or 0.0625 ha (25 by 25 m) and survey teams can walk their paths at 10–25 m spacing. This slows down the fieldwork, so it either takes longer and costs more or the total area surveyed is smaller. There is no one correct spatial resolution to work at; it depends on the region, the nature of its archaeological record, and the nature of the research questions and the degree of precision required of the demographic data needed to answer them.

This methodology could divide the site in Figure 5.1 into 11 collection units of 0.25 ha or 37 units of 0.0625 ha. These are shown in Figure 5.3 as they might plausibly be drawn with careful attention in the field—bounded both by the observed outer limits of the artifact scatter and, within it, somewhat more arbitrarily by field boundaries, roads, or other landscape features (especially ones that might become meaningful boundaries between occupied and unoccupied areas for particular periods). A few very scattered artifacts at the east edge of the figure have gone unnoticed, as well might occur in the field. The smaller collection units, obviously, give greater spatial resolution—especially considering the way in which these either would or would not be included in the total area calculated for different periods of occupation, depending on which collection units yielded materials of different periods.

Perhaps not so intuitively obvious, the two sizes of collection units give different calculations of total area: 2.4 ha for the larger collections units and 2.0 ha for the smaller. The greater spatial precision of the smaller collection units identifies and excludes from consideration small gaps in the artifact scatter that the larger collection units tend simply to gloss over and include

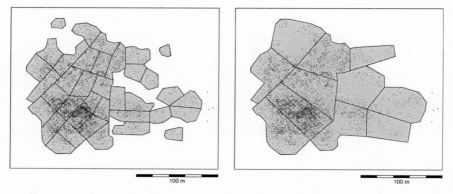

Figure 5.3. The artifact scatter from Figure 5.1 divided into collection units 0.0625 ha each (left) and 0.25 ha each (right).

in the overall occupied area. This sort of variation in area measurements from collection units of different sizes has shown up quite clearly in some comparative analyses, where it must be taken into account to maintain the validity of the comparison.

Points and Pitfalls

Especially since economical hand-held GPS units have come into wide-spread use, another approach to recording areas in the field has become increasingly common. It springs from a substantially different conceptual-ization of data recording and analysis—one that might be referred to as "point-think" in contrast to the "area-think" represented above. Area-think derives directly from the methodology developed in the Basin of Mexico to characterize areas of surface artifact distribution without attempting the obviously impossible mapping of all individual artifact locations across thousands of square kilometers. Point-think springs from the same con-cern for detailed but efficient recording of artifact distributions.

Instead of envisioning a region as divided into small areas or polygons, point-think imagines a regular grid of points across the region as locations at each of which an artifact collection will be made. If the same artifact scat-ter we have been looking at were recorded as surface collections made in 5 x 5 m squares in a grid of points spaced 25 m apart, the result would be as shown in Figure 5.4 (upper left). Figure 5.4 (upper right) shows how these results could be used to draw boundaries around the occupied area, by making boundary lines that fall halfway between points where collec-tions yielded artifacts and points where collections yielded nothing. The area would be measured at 1.8 ha, not wildly different from the measure-

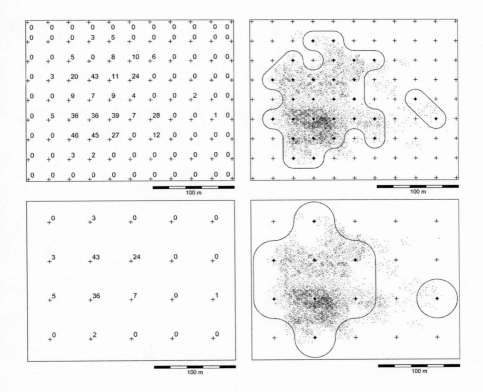

Figure 5.4. The results of recording the artifact scatter from Figure 5.1 as collections in 5 x 5 m squares at 25 m intervals (above) and 50 m intervals (below). The numbers of artifacts from each collection are shown at left, and these numbers are the basis for delimiting the artifact scatter at right.

ment based on collection units 25 x 25 m, although the boundaries are a crude representation of the limits of the scatter—both including some areas devoid of artifacts and excluding a substantial amount of low-density scatter. If the interval between point-based collections is increased to 50 m, the area measures 2.1 ha and its boundaries are drawn even more crudely as in Figure 5.4 (lower right). Low-density portions of the scatter are again excluded and still larger areas without artifacts are included.

The differences between area-based collection units and point-based collections are much more dramatic in dispersed surface distributions of low density. Figure 5.5 shows the same four approaches to recording, this time carried out in an extensive low-density scatter. Only a few isolated artifacts are omitted from collection units of 0.0625 ha; margins of the scatter would be fairly tightly delimited; and the total area of occupation is measured at 1.9 ha. Collection units of 0.25 ha would be more approximate and expansive about limits and identify fewer gaps in the distribution, measuring the total occupied area at 3.2 ha. Point-based collections at 25 m intervals would very often encounter no artifacts, even though at least some could be observed nearby. A total of 0.5 ha is measured for several diminutive areas that are non-contiguous but not far apart. Based on the point collection data, it would be difficult to decide just how to treat this evidence of occupation. Much the same could be said of point-based collections at 50 m intervals; the area would be measured at 1.1 ha.

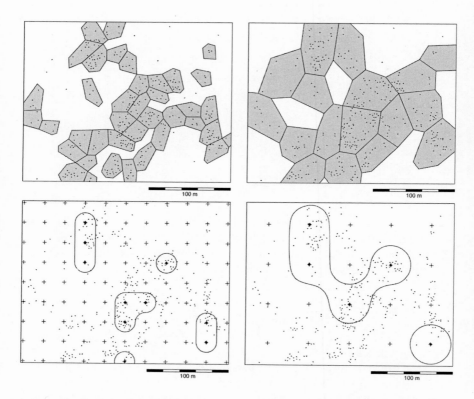

Figure 5.5. The results of recording a dispersed low-density artifact scatter in collection units of 0.0625 ha (upper left), collection units of 0.25 ha (upper right), collections in 5 x 5 m squares at 25 m intervals (lower left) and collections in 5 x 5 m squares at 50 m intervals (lower right). The artifact scatter is a real one, in this case lithics from sparse hunter-gatherer occupations, but sherd distributions in zones of dispersed farmsteads can have these same characteristics. (Data from Drager and Ireland 1986.)

GPS units have also been used to map individual artifacts in place along transects walked by survey teams, amounting to a sort of "line-think." Archaeology around the Mediterranean has been a particularly rich source of other variants of point-think and line-think, although the scale referred to as regional in these studies is almost always much smaller than that emphasized in this book, and many of the methods developed record a level of detail that would be prohibitively expensive (as well as unnecessary) on a scale of several tens of square kilometers or more.

Making surface collections in delimited areas on a grid of points or lines has strong appeal, to judge from the number of projects that collect data in this way. It does not involve subjective judgments on the part of survey team members; they simply go to the coordinates of the next point on the list as indicated by their GPS unit and make another collection. This ensures quick training of field crews and consistency across different teams. The rigidity and regularity of a grid of points across a region is especially appealing to some people (at least when they overlook the fact that the regularity is only in where the GPS units *say* the points are, which will really be off by 5–10 m or more in the field). This rigidity and regularity works in flat, relatively undifferentiated landscapes; it could be a nightmare in the mountains. The scheme could be adapted to uneven terrain, though, by locating collection points in convenient positions at approximately the desired interval and recording these locations (whatever they are). In such areas, however, topography might largely preclude occupation between two points where artifacts are found, although this information would not become part of the dataset.

Point-based collections are open to more sources of random noise since the spaces around the point locations of collections are characterized by the luck of what happens to be within the collection area at a given point. Approaching a landscape in terms of area-based collection units places greater emphasis on active observation by fieldworkers who make more subjective judgments. They ramble around on artifact scatters, incorporating into boundary delimitation whatever they can observe—anywhere and everywhere—about scatter limits, varying artifact densities, internal gaps, associated architecture and features, etc. Areas where the characteristics of the surface assemblage appear to differ can be separated into different collection units. Data recording by collection units provides for more accurate delineation of the boundaries of surface scatters and thus more precise measurements of their areas. Although we haven't discussed it, information on architectural remains or other features visible on the surface is easy to record, collection unit by collection unit.

Although rather different measurements of occupied area were produced by the different methods in the examples here, survey results produced by any one of them could be internally consistent. The different modes of measurement, however, would become a serious concern to be dealt with in comparative analysis between regions where the areas were not measured in the same way. It may come as a surprise that something as conceptually simple as area of surface scatter could be measured in so many incompatible ways, each of which was nonetheless a perfectly reasonable and consistent mode of measurement—at least under some circumstances.

Where artifact densities are high and surface visibility is good, area-based collection units and collections made at closely spaced point locations in a grid may yield fairly similar results—although area-based collection units facilitate mapping scatter limits where they are observed to be, rather than at some indeterminate position (usually halfway) between a collection that yields artifacts and the next one that doesn't. Where artifact densities are low and/or surface visibility is poor, collections made at point locations in a grid are increasingly subject to random noise, because it is increasingly likely that no artifacts will be visible at the designated point location even though they may be observed en route to that location.

Area-based collection units naturally take architectural remains, topographic detail, and other observations into account in delimiting scatters. For example, when artifacts are concentrated on a relatively level hilltop that slopes off sharply on all sides, this topographic detail can guide the delimitation of the area likely to have been occupied if those limits are drawn in the field with the topography under direct observation. Under most circumstances area-based collection units provide more detailed and accurate delimitation of occupied areas because they make it possible to rely on more sources of information. Their advantages in this regard increase at low artifact densities and in conditions of relatively low surface visibility. In our experience area-think leads to both better data recovery and greater efficiency. When surface visibility is extremely poor, however, there may be no alternative but to resort to collections at grid intervals utilizing some form of subsurface sampling. And this brings us directly to the subjects of the next two sections.

MEASURING DENSITY OF MATERIALS IN THE FIELD

Making collections of artifacts has been referred to only vaguely thus far, with little attention to just how this is done. Surface collections are made for a variety of reasons, but measuring the density of surface materials well sets some of the most stringent methodological requirements, so we will discuss collecting methods in that context.

Systematic Collections

If surface collections are made at point locations in a grid, there is little more to say about the locations where collections are made; the grid of points determines them. At each point location, an area of some predetermined size is marked off and the artifacts within it are collected, bagged, tagged, and returned to the lab for cleaning and analysis. A quick and easy way to mark off an area for collection is by drawing a dog-leash circle. One team member stands on the selected center point holding one end of a rope, while another team member holding the other end of the rope circles around, marking a circle on the ground with a foot or a pointed stick. Squares can also be used but it takes longer in the field to mark one off. It makes it easier to think of and work with densities if the circle size provides for some even number of square meters, say a 1.78 m dog-leash radius for a circle of 10 m^2 or a 2.82 m radius for a circle of 25 m^2. In any event, the number of sherds collected divided by the area marked off for collection gives a numeric density value in sherds/m^2 for that point location.

If the survey is organized by collection unit polygons, there are more decisions to make. In areas of relatively high surface density, it is not practical to collect all the artifacts from an entire area of 0.0625 ha (equivalent to 25 by 25 m), much less of 0.25 ha or 1 ha. Dog-leash circles can be used to demarcate areas of known size somewhere within the collection units, and the collections made from these dog-leash circles can be taken to represent the average density and nature of artifacts not just for the dog-leash circles themselves, but for the entire area of the collection unit. Thus collections from the dog-leash circles are samples from the universe of all artifacts in the collection unit polygons they will represent, and consideration of good sampling design can help achieve better results from these collections. The aim of good sampling design in this context would be to get a sample of artifacts that is (a) large enough to characterize the assemblage of artifacts in the collection unit with sufficient precision and confidence and (b) selected in such as way as to minimize sampling bias (that is, maximize the chance of representing the universe accurately).

How large a sample has to be depends on what you need to say about the universe it represents. One fundamental thing we need to determine is the proportions of sherds of different periods in a collection unit, since these proportions are the basis for establishing the density of materials of the different periods. The precision and confidence with which samples of different sizes enable us to make this determination is a simple and straightforward statistical question. A sample of 384 sherds will give us 95% confidence in saying what proportion of all the sherds in a collection unit those of a particular period represent, within an error range of ±5%. This is a lot of sherds to collect (and carry home) from each of the thousands of collection units a regional survey might record, not to mention that there might not be 384 sherds on the entire surface of the collection unit (a point we will return to below).

Regional surveys usually accept lower confidence levels and larger error ranges, and experience indicates that this can be done without introducing unacceptable amounts of random noise into the survey data. If we lower our standards to 80% confidence and an error range of ±10%, for example, a sample of 41 will suffice. The target sample size has one simple and direct implication for the size of the dog-leash circle, if that is how the artifacts will be collected. In an artifact scatter where the overall density of ceramics is about 4 sherds/m^2, a dog-leash circle covering 10 m^2 will generally yield around 40 sherds. This size circle, then, would be a pretty good match for a target sample of 41. In collection units with lower densities of surface materials, we might mark off larger circles, but it turns out to be better to mark off additional circles for collection until a sample of the target size was obtained.

This statistical basis for deciding how many artifacts need to be collected takes the collection to be a simple random sample of the artifacts in the collection unit. If the artifact sample is collected by drawing a dog-leash circle in the middle of a collection unit and picking up all the artifacts in the circle, then it is not technically a simple random sample of, say, 41 sherds, but a spatially based cluster sample of one circle. This would lead us to calculate the error ranges and confidence levels somewhat differently, but we don't in fact calculate such error ranges for the sample from each collection unit. The aim of the previous paragraph is simply to recognize that random noise is greater in small samples, and this provides a useful approach to thinking about how many sherds we'd like to have from each collection unit in order to keep random noise down to acceptable levels. Random noise is also greater if the entire sample comes from one selected place in the collection unit. If the sample is obtained from a number of different locations within the collection unit, then it is more likely to accurately represent the overall artifact assemblage of the collection unit, because it will more effectively tap the variation in density and proportional composition of the assemblage that we would expect to occur across the space encompassed by the collection unit.

An actual example of varying densities across a collection unit of 0.25 ha is shown in Figure 5.6. The overall average sherd density for the entire collection unit is 2.0 sherds/m^2. If we attempted to measure this density by selecting one location at random for a dog-leash circle of 5 m^2, we could get a wide variety of results, ranging from a low of 0.6 to a high of 4.6 sherds/m^2. About 80% of the time our measurement would be somewhere between 0.9 and 3.1 sherds/m^2. If instead of collecting a single circle, we always selected four adjacent circles and averaged the result, we would come closer more often. About 80% of the time our measurement would be between 1.3 and 3.2 sherds/m^2. This improvement is not dramatic, and mostly it comes from increasing the size of the sample; four adjacent circles still tap into very little more of the density variation across the collection unit than a single circle did.

The best way to encompass more of that density variation across the collection unit, so as to obtain even more precise measurements, is to scat-

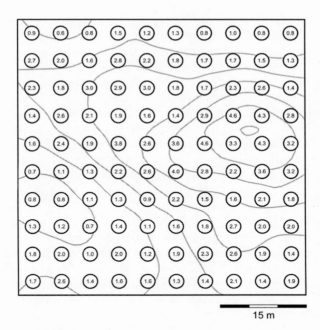

Figure 5.6. An artifact scatter within a collection unit of exactly 0.25 ha based on an actual distribution of Hongshan period artifacts in the Upper Daling region. Gray contour lines show the trends of changing sherd density across the collection unit. Dog-leash circles, each covering 5 m², are shown all across the collection unit, with the densities of sherds/m² each would contain.

ter the dog-leash circles farther apart. If we make collections again in four circles, but instead of adjacent circles we randomly select a circle from each quarter of the collection unit (northwest, northeast, southeast, and southwest), random noise is substantially reduced: 80% of the time our measurement would be between 1.5 and 2.5 sherds/m². The same kind of reduction in random noise in the data would be expected in assessing the proportions of the sherds that pertain to each period or to other categories.

Putting together these thoughts about sampling the artifact assemblage variability across a collection unit polygon can lead to simple, efficient field strategies that minimize the amount of random noise. If we decide that we would like measurements of the proportions of sherds of different periods to have error ranges no greater than ±8% at the 80% confidence level, we would establish 64 as the target size for the sherd sample from each collection unit. If relatively high-density scatters in the region to be surveyed have densities of 3–4 sherds/m², then we might begin collecting with two dog-leash circles of 10 m² each (1.78 m radius) in two different parts of the collection unit. In high-density scatters these would usually yield 60–80 sherds and thus satisfy, or almost satisfy, the target size of 64 for the sherd sample. The two circles in two different parts of the collection unit would provide two separate observations of the density for averaging together, reducing random noise in the dataset—although not by quite as much as four circles would. On the other hand, the number of sherds would usually be large, reducing random noise from that source somewhat more than our goal. If 64 sherds were not obtained, then another dog-leash circle would be collected in a third different part of the collection unit. If 64 sherds had still not been obtained (as would be the case in lower-density scatters), yet another circle would be collected, and so on. As long as the number of circles collected is always recorded, then the actual density of sherds/m^2 can be calculated for each collection unit without collecting far more sherds than are needed in some collection units and too few in others.

A procedure like this makes good sense—for some specific contexts at least—in striking a balance between time invested and random noise reduction. Most important, it avoids sampling bias. The numbers for target sample size, area and number of circles, and so on would differ depending on the specifics of the region, the archaeological record, the research questions to be answered, and other factors.

General Collections

The procedure is still incomplete, however, in one important way. Even in regions where surface densities reach 3 or 4 sherds/m^2 or much higher, there are sometimes collection units with far lower densities. Here the effort to collect 64 sherds would require marking off circle after circle all day long, and at the end of the day it could turn out that there are simply not 64 sherds on the surface in the entire collection unit. This definitely is not an efficient use of time. A different procedure must be applied to collection units at the low end of the density scale. If the surface density in a collection unit is as low as 1 sherd/m^2, then it would take around six dog-leash circles of 10 m^2 each to approach the target sample size of 64 sherds. This sounds like the point of diminishing returns for marking off circles to measure the sherd density in a single collection unit. One might, then, make a quick subjective estimate of the sherd density at the very beginning of work in a collection unit. If the density appeared to be less than 1 sherd/m^2, then no circles would be drawn at all. Instead members of the survey team would roam the survey unit collecting the artifacts they saw until the target number of 64 had been obtained (or until some fixed time limit had been reached). Such helter-skelter collections have sometimes been referred to as "grab samples" or "general" collections, in contrast to "systematic" or "controlled" collections in marked-off circles or squares.

If general collections of this sort are made where densities are low, then uniformly low density values can be assigned to those collection units. We could reason that general collections were only made in the above example where densities were judged to be less than 1 sherd/m^2 and they might well be substantially below that level. We could assign a density of 0.5 sherds/m^2 to collection units where general collections were made. Or we might go even further and recognize that in some low-density collection units even fewer than 64 sherds would be recovered. We might assign a density of 0.75 sherds/m^2 to collection units where 60 sherds or more were recovered; of 0.50 sherds/m^2 where 30–59 sherds were recovered; and of 0.25 sherds/m^2 where fewer than 30 sherds could be found. If we followed this path, we would probably want to limit the time for making a general collection to, say, 10 minutes to make sure that a team didn't just spend a very long time hunting sherds in one unit. Survey teams must pick up whatever sherds they see, making sure not to introduce sampling bias by (for example) picking up all the rare early or decorated sherds and only some of the more abundant later or plain sherds. Once both the area and the surface density of a collection unit have been measured, the two necessary elements for an area-density index are in hand.

This may sound like a complex and cumbersome set of procedures for surface collecting, but the complexity comes from the flexibility of adjusting the procedure to the varying conditions encountered in different collection units, so as to be efficient in arriving at a reasonably accurate measured or subjectively judged surface artifact density for each collection unit. If densities really vary little from one collection unit to another in a region, or if surface conditions like vegetation make surface densities impossible to measure well, then it may make sense to concentrate on measuring the areas of scatters and use area as the population proxy—thus saving time by not attempting to measure densities. In such a case, general collections are made in all collection units.

Many projects make only general collections and record subjective judgments of the density in each collection unit. In these cases analysis is likely to assign a population range to each category and then an absolute population estimate to each collection unit based on its area and subjectively judged density (essentially as was done in the Basin of Mexico). A number of experienced surveyors have avoided systematic collections for fear of slowing down the work; a number of others who have used them find that they add little time to the process of recording data on a collection unit. Procedures like those just described for measuring densities with systematic collections in high-density collection units, and general collections in low-density collection units, have been used in surveys that achieved the coverage rate cited above of about 1 km^2 per day for a three-person team.

It is worth noting in conclusion that archaeological sites have not played a role as units of data recording or analysis in any of the methods recommended here for measuring occupied areas and densities of surface materials. These methods entirely avoid the sometimes unwarranted assumptions of tight clusters of remains, separated by areas completely devoid of them, that are inherent in using sites as the fundamental units of data recording and analysis. They provide an accurate and efficient way of recording detailed information about the distribution of artifacts on a regional scale that will reveal patterns ranging from highly dispersed farmsteads or even mobile occupations to the compact, nucleated local communities that correspond one-for-one to what archaeologists have always called "sites."

DEALING WITH POOR SURFACE VISIBILITY IN THE FIELD

The discussion of measuring areas of occupation and densities of materials up to this point has assumed that conditions make artifacts on the surface readily visible, and regional survey and settlement demography have thrived in a number of regions where conditions for it are propitious. Such research has also been successful where conditions are much less favorable and additional successes have been achieved where conditions for surface survey are indescribably bad. Very often the culprit is vegetation: high forest, thick leaf litter, heavy brush, the thick sod of grazing areas.

In at least some of these circumstances, regional survey has relied on rapid shovel testing. Although not without its critics, shovel testing has been extensively employed in areas of poor surface visibility. Field methods usually resemble making controlled surface collections at each point in a regular grid of points (as described above). The only difference is that in place of a surface collection, a small test is excavated. These shovel tests or shovel probes are usually 1 x 1 m or smaller. Sometimes they are excavated down to sterile subsoil, sometimes to a fixed depth. The soil is either examined by hand or screened to recover artifacts.

Areas of occupation are determined by drawing their limits around probes that yielded artifacts, often separating occupied territory from unoccupied territory at the midpoint between probes that yielded artifacts and those that didn't (as in the examples above of surface collections at regular grids of points). Densities of materials are sometimes calculated in terms of surface area (a shovel probe 50 x 50 cm that yields 4 sherds represents a density of 16 sherds/m^2) or sometimes volumetrically (a shovel probe 50 x 50 cm and 40 cm deep that yields 4 sherds represents a density of 40 sherds/m^3). Much of what can be said about controlled surface collection at a regular grid of points also applies to digging shovel tests at a regular grid of points. In particular, there is a risk of finding no artifacts at that particular point even in a zone of occupation. Since shovel probes are smaller than controlled surface collection areas, this risk is greater for shovel probes. For both surface collections and shovel probes, this risk increases dramatically under conditions of low artifact density within occupied areas.

In the Alto Magdalena, shovel probes were combined with surface collection in an approach founded not on a grid of point locations, but rather on the area-think of small collection unit polygons as the basic unit of data recording. Survey proceeded collection unit by collection unit, making surface collections (or noting the absence of artifacts) where conditions provided acceptable surface visibility. Where vegetation prevented adequate surface visibility, shovel probes were dug to see whether a patch of ground that could become a collection unit had artifacts or not, and to recover an artifact sample if they were present. This procedure made it possible to incorporate topographic and other indications of plausible boundaries of occupied areas in the delimitation of collection units, and their limits were drawn on paper copies of aerial photographs. A single shovel probe was taken to represent each collection unit, but it would have been better (though slower) to dig several shovel probes in each collection unit—as described above for dog-leash circles—to combat both random noise in density measurements and the risk of shovel probes that failed to find artifacts, even though they were present in low density in the collection unit.

If density measures from shovel probes and surface collections are to be integrated in a single dataset, some sort of equivalence between the two measures must be established. At El Hatillo in Panama, shovel probes and surface collections were paired in each of a sample of collection units so as to establish a conversion factor from the paired data. In the Tonosí region, the shapes of the frequency distributions of sherd densities from shovel probes and surface collections were aligned after arguing that the two could be treated as random samples from the same universe.

SAMPLING IN THE FIELD

The use of sampling in regional survey is a controversial topic, perhaps especially among those who have most clearly recognized the full extent to which the aims of regional settlement analysis are fundamentally demographic in nature. Sampling has found a comfortable niche in cultural resource surveys at a wide variety of scales in the United States and Canada. It has also received explicit attention around the Mediterranean, usually at scales far smaller than the regions this book focuses on. The literature on the subject contains a number of experiments to see what a sampling scheme would have found if applied to a region for which the data from a full coverage survey are available. The majority of these experiments try out badly designed sampling schemes; the most common error is to choose sampling units that are far too large, resulting in a sample size (n) that is far too small.

This point can be illustrated quickly by applying two sampling schemes to the fully surveyed western zone of the Valle de la Plata; at the same time, we can explore what could be accomplished with a well-designed sample of the region. A small size (1 ha) was chosen for the quadrat units of the first sample (Figure 5.7) so that the sample could have a large number of units (1,283). The complete survey area covers 317.24 km², so the 12.83 km² total of the sample quadrats amounts to a sampling fraction of 4% (a much smaller sampling fraction than in most published "tests" of the performance of samples in regional survey). The important thing, though, is the sample size (*n*), which at 1,283 is much larger than in most published efforts of this kind.

The sample quadrats were laid out on a regular grid at a spacing of 500 m. There are many, sometimes conflicting, opinions on the best way to select a spatial sample. Systematic designs like this one spread the sample broadly across the region, avoiding sample units that clump together as well as large areas that go unsampled. This is an intuitively appealing thing to accomplish in spatial sampling and there is theoretical reason to believe that it does improve results, since spatial autocorrelation makes closely spaced units somewhat redundant and large unsampled areas a particularly worrisome source of error. Some systematic designs avoid the regular spacing and alignment of these sample units, but in this mountainous

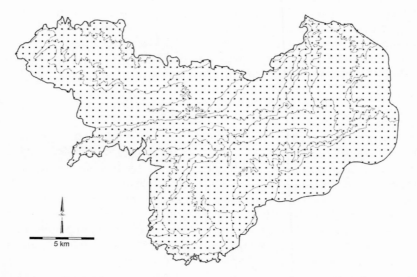

Figure 5.7. A sample of 1,283 quadrats of 1 ha each in the western survey zone of the Valle de la Plata. Within the survey area, the soil productivity zones discussed in the text are indicated. (Data from Drennan 2006a, 2006b.)

region there seems little reason to worry that the even spacing or alignment of sampling units might match patterns in the settlement distribution in unfortunate ways.

Since density was uniformly low and very difficult to measure for all
collection units in the Valle de la Plata, the population proxy used was area.
Overall population estimates for the region are thus a simple question of
estimating the mean occupied area per hectare in the survey area from the
1 ha sample units. For each period the occupied area falling in each 1 ha
sample quadrat was measured from the complete survey data and the
mean and standard error were calculated across all 1,283 sample units. The
sample results represent the full dataset very accurately right through
the sequence, with quite a narrow error range at the 95% confidence level
(Figure 5.8).

In Chapter 3 we looked at the relationship between population and
agricultural productivity for 13 soil zones in this same survey area and discovered a negative correlation of moderate strength and high significance
($r_s = -0.680, p = 0.011, n = 13$) for the Formative 1 period. Precisely the same
approach can be taken with the sample data (by estimating the area occupied separately for each soil zone) and the result supports the same conclusion ($r_s = -0.600, p = 0.030, n = 13$). For the Regional Classic period, the

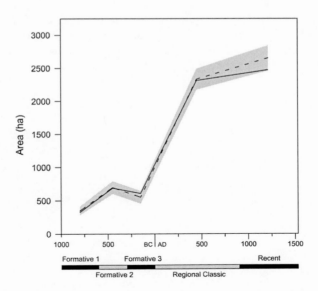

Figure 5.8. Total occupied area in the western survey zone of the Valle de la Plata
as estimated from the sample in Figure 5.7 (dashed line, with gray error zone for
95% confidence) compared with the total from the complete dataset (solid line).

full dataset indicates a weak positive relationship of not much significance between population and the 13 soil productivity zones ($r_s = 0.345, p = 0.248, n = 13$). Again, analysis of the sample leads to precisely the same conclusion ($r_s = 0.229, p = 0.451, n = 13$).

The sample would not provide the basis for a rank-size graph—but then neither would the complete survey, because the dispersed farmstead occupation simply did not include the local communities needed as analytical units for rank-size graphs. A centralization analysis based on concentric rings could be carried out, using the estimated area of occupation in each ring from the sample. Even representing the general trends in population distribution as a smoothed density surface shows highly similar results between the entire dataset and the sample (Figure 5.9). Both principal population concentrations are easily seen, as are some of the fragmentary smaller ones at the margins of the survey area. Supra-local communities would be defined in essentially the same way for both the sample and the entire dataset, because the more sparsely occupied buffer zones between them are well captured by the sample.

The same survey region could also be sampled less skillfully with quadrats of 1 km² (Figure 5.10). For such large quadrats, boundary issues arise since some potential sample quadrats will have substantial areas both inside and outside the survey area. To handle this consistently, the universe sampled was expanded to a total area of 364 km² to include all 1 km² quadrats in the grid that were not completely outside the survey boundaries. A total of fifteen 1 km² quadrats was randomly selected from these 364, for a sampling fraction of 4.1%. The sampling fraction is slightly larger than for the sample of 1 ha quadrats, but this is not very important. What really matters is that the black magic of poor sampling design has traded

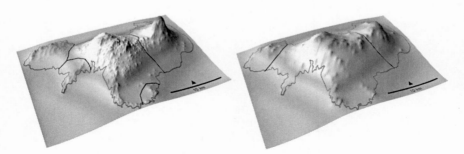

Figure 5.9. Smoothed surface representing population distribution in the western survey zone of the Valle de la Plata based on the entire survey dataset (left) and based on the sample from Figure 5.7 (right). Division of demographic clusters into supra-local communities is shown on both surfaces.

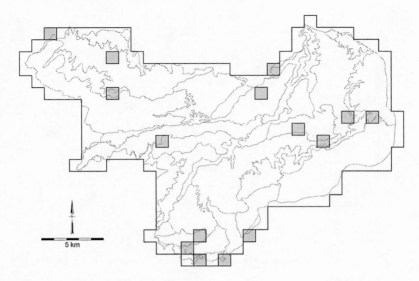

Figure 5.10. A sample of 15 quadrats of 1 km² each in the western survey zone of the Valle de la Plata. These were chosen from the universe indicated by the rectilinear border outside the boundaries of the survey zone. (Data from Drennan 2006a, 2006b.)

in a sample size (n) of 1,283 for one of 15. The systematic design that spread the 1 ha quadrats evenly across the survey region has also been abandoned for a simple random design that allows several sample units to cluster together and leaves very large tracts unsampled.

Not surprisingly, this sample does not do a very good job of estimating occupied area in the region through time (Figure 5.11). It would do a similarly poor job at all the other analyses. This sampling design has much in common with some published examples, one of which uses 1 km² quadrats as its *smallest* size and works its way up from there to a sample with $n = 4$. The poor outcomes of such experiments do not show that sampling doesn't work well; they only show that poorly designed sampling doesn't work well.

When Is Sampling Better?

A persistent practical worry about sampling schemes is that it would take just as much time to get to scattered sample quadrats and survey them as it would to just survey the entire region completely. This was not the experience in the Valle de la Plata. After a small part of the eastern survey zone had been covered completely, it began to appear that there was very

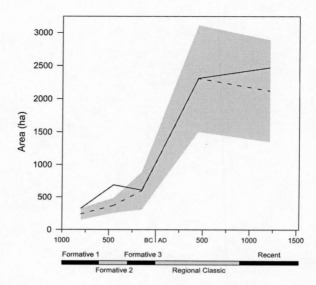

Figure 5.11. Total occupied area in the western survey zone of the Valle de la Plata as estimated from the sample in Figure 5.10 (dashed line, with gray error zone for 95% confidence) compared to the total from the complete dataset (solid line).

little pre-Hispanic occupation there in any period (especially compared with the western zone, which had already been partly surveyed). It seemed risky, however, to make this conclusion based on one fully surveyed small sector of a much more extensive environmental zone. At the same time, it was discouraging to think of investing time in complete survey of a substantially larger region from which the anticipated conclusion was simply that there was very little occupation in any pre-Hispanic period.

The strategy selected was to sample that much larger zone with 1 ha quadrats. The sample results produced high confidence that pre-Hispanic occupation was never substantial in any part of this eastern zone. It demonstrated that this settlement consisted of isolated farmsteads and very small groups of farmsteads, because all occupied areas discovered in sample quadrats were explored and recorded in their entirety to determine just how extensive were contiguous areas of occupation. The sample also revealed that occupation was very strongly oriented toward permanent water sources (not surprising for a very dry region). Sampling was efficient: survey teams sampled the area in about one-fourth the time that would have been required for complete survey. Thus, given the time invested, the sample survey in the eastern zone covered an area four times as large as complete survey could have.

By contrast, despite the success of the above sampling experiment with 1,283 1 ha quadrats for the western survey zone of the Valle de la Plata, the original decision to carry out complete survey there seems wise. It led more directly to important observations than a sample would have. It would, for instance, have been more difficult to make the unexpected observation that occupation throughout the pre-Hispanic sequence consisted not of nucleated villages, but of very dispersed farmsteads. Such fundamentally unexpected observations do not come as readily from samples. This is especially true of observations arrived at by just looking at maps to see what patterns are there (although a density surface produced from a sample can certainly document some such things, as shown in Figure 5.9).

Complete survey of the western zone of the Valle de la Plata provided a sound beginning for regional settlement demography in the Alto Magdalena at a time when nothing was known of settlement or population patterns there (Figure 5.12). Subsequently, sampling the eastern zone saved resources and found out what needed to be found out. The small central

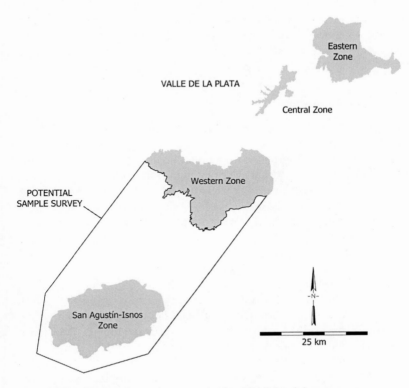

Figure 5.12. Regional survey zones in the Alto Magdalena.

zone was surveyed completely to document the nature of the transition between the very different environmental and demographic conditions to the
west and east of it. Finally, the San Agustín–Isnos zone was surveyed completely. With the resources expended on the complete survey of the 323 km²
San Agustín–Isnos zone, it would have been possible instead to sample the
much larger zone indicated in Figure 5.12 with 1 ha quadrats in a design
similar to the experimental sampling of the western zone of the Valle de la
Plata discussed above. There is a case to be made that this would have produced more useful knowledge about ancient settlement demography in
the Alto Magdalena. Prior knowledge from the Valle de la Plata survey
would have made it possible to design and evaluate sampling strategies
on a settlement distribution with characteristics similar to the one to be
sampled.

A sample of the larger area would have encompassed practically the
entire zone of monumental tombs and statues that are the defining features
of the "San Agustín culture." The conclusion that the entire region was organized into perhaps a dozen small polities of similar size would be on
sounder footing than it is now, because they would virtually all have been
included in the analysis—or, alternatively, a sparsely occupied buffer zone
between a few polities in the western Valle de la Plata and a few in the San
Agustín–Isnos zone might have been discovered. If such a zone were present, it would suggest a separation of regional polities into different groups
and hitherto unsuspected structure at an even larger spatial scale.

Sampling Under Sediments

Up to this point, we have not considered the possibility that the landscape
occupied by the people we want to study may have been so altered by
geological processes—like erosion and deposition—that it is simply no
longer accessible to observation at or near the surface. Some of the classic
archaeological cases of early complex societies, however, occupy large flat
floodplains where substantial amounts of sediment have been deposited
since these societies existed. Particularly in the broad plains of central and
southern China, archaeologists have had considerable success finding and
documenting areas of occupation buried under 10 m or more of sterile sediments by coring with soil augers. Cultural materials have been recovered
and anthropogenic soils recognized in auger holes with diameters around
10 cm. Coring is laborious but certainly within the realm of possibility on
a large scale. In the Chengdu Plain of southern China, cultural materials
were usually not buried by more than 2 m of sediment, but Rowan Flad
reports that eight people working in the field for one month can dig some
2,400 auger holes to this depth.

The Upper Daling region in northeastern China is not buried by sediment and its complete survey provides the opportunity for another

experiment in sampling, this time imagining that the entire settlement distribution across these 200 km² was buried under some 2 m of more recent sediment and discoverable only by augering. A sample of 3,197 point locations for cores was selected in the same way as the 1 ha sample quadrats in the Valle de la Plata sampling experiment—as a regular grid of points, this time at a spacing of 250 m (Figure 5.13). For each period the number of points that hit an occupation of that period, as documented in the complete survey data, was divided by 3,197 to calculate the proportion of the point sample that fell within an occupied area. This amounts to a sampling estimate of the proportion of all the possible points in the survey area that fall within occupied areas for the period; an error range for the estimate can be produced from standard sampling statistics for any desired confidence level. When this proportion and its error range are multiplied by the total of 200 km² in the survey area, the result is an estimate of the total occupied area for that period with an error range for the specified confidence level. This sample yields a graph of changing occupied area through time in the Upper Daling region (Figure 5.14) that agrees well with the one from the full dataset, with a fairly narrow error range for the 95% confidence level.

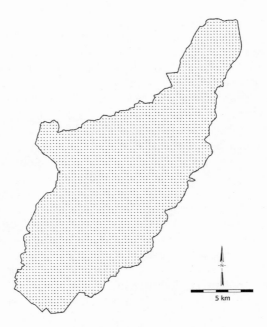

Figure 5.13. A sample of point locations for auger cores at 250 m spacing in the Upper Daling region. (Data from Peterson et al. 2014a, 2014b.)

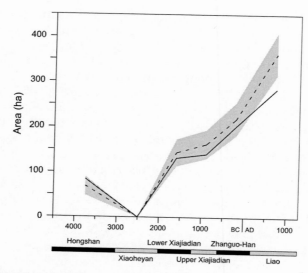

Figure 5.14. Total occupied area in the Upper Daling region as estimated from the sample in Figure 5.13 (dashed line, with gray error zone for 95% confidence) compared to the total from the complete dataset (solid line).

An area-density index was actually a better population proxy for the Upper Daling region than just area alone. A core sample will not likely produce a very good estimate of densities at the locations it discovers, because an auger hole represents such a small area. Indeed, the small size of an auger hole may create substantial risk of failing to recover cultural material in one even though it falls within an occupied area. This has led some to dig several auger holes at each selected location instead of just one so as to increase the volume of sediment sampled. This practice can materially reduce the risk of missing an occupation, but it is unlikely that it would estimate the density of materials at each location (or, for that matter, the proportions of sherds of different periods there) with much precision.

A two-stage coring strategy will probably work better. That is, an initial sample of cores at point locations could be followed by grids of more closely spaced cores at each positive location to delimit the contiguous area of occupation there. These cores might be placed at intervals of, say, 25 m, 50 m, or 100 m, depending on the area and density of the occupations in the region and the precision of delimitation needed to answer the research questions that led to the project in the first place. In many areas of occupation, this would amount to enough auger holes to make possible more accurate estimates of densities of materials and proportions of materials of different periods in that location as well. Estimates of this sort could then be used to refine the initial estimates of total occupied area for the region into a more fully satisfactory population proxy. It is of course important that sampling estimates be based on only the data collected in the first-stage random sample; the additional data from the second stage cannot simply be thrown together with the first-stage data as a sample from the region. This is because the second stage has a very strong bias in favor of locations already known to have cultural materials, and will thus unrealistically inflate estimates of how much cultural material there is in the region and how it is distributed.

The complete survey of the Upper Daling region was carried out in about six weeks by some 15 archaeologists and archaeology students. If four auger holes 1–2 m deep were made at each of the 3,197 point locations in the core sample imagined above, it might have required about twice as much investment of time as the complete surface survey, although not all members of the field team would need as much archaeological training for the augering. Further coring to delimit occupations discovered would add to that, but certainly not put it out of the realm of possibility for an archaeological project.

A two-stage strategy of coring at widely scattered locations followed by coring at closer intervals—to provide more detail about occupations discovered—would be more effective and efficient than attempting to combine both objectives into a single stage. Lines of cores at close spacing have sometimes been used to sample right across a region along one or a few chosen transects, at an interval small enough to prevent sites being missed because they fell between cores. Purposefully chosen lines of cores, however, do not make a good sampling design because they leave very large areas that might be quite different from each other entirely unsampled. Technically, the size of the sample is not the number of cores but the number of lines, and the purposeful selection of lines almost certainly introduces sampling bias. A full grid of point locations, in contrast, does provide a sound statistical basis for estimating parameters for the region as a whole. If the alignment of cores within a grid is a worry, then instead of cores at regular 250 m spacing, a point location can be selected randomly within each 250 m quadrat in the grid.

The distinction between complete coverage and sampling, so seemingly simple in the abstract, is actually very complicated in real space. We have treated cores at 250 m intervals as a sample. It is nonetheless accurate to say that it represents complete coverage with respect to sites more than about 250 m across, since no such site can be missed. The Valle de la Plata sample of 1 ha quadrats at 500 m spacing could likewise be considered full coverage with respect to sites more than about 500 m across. Once the interval between the lines walked by surface surveyors is down to 100 m or less, the survey is usually called full or complete coverage and not thought of as a sample. This is true with respect to sites more than about 100 m across, but of course not with respect to sites 50 m across. A full coverage survey with surveyors walking lines about 100 m apart will discover only a sample of the sites 50 m across. There is no reason not to combine sampling estimates about sites 50 m across from such a survey with the complete data about sites larger than 100 m across, although we are not aware that anyone has actually done this.

SOME QUESTIONS AND ANSWERS

1. Survey crews sometimes seem to have an irresistible urge to hunt around a collection unit for a place with as many artifacts as they can find and mark their dog-leash circle there for making a systematic collection. Why should you try to avoid this? How can you avoid it?

The aim of making small careful systematic collections in dog-leash circles within larger collection unit areas is to get an accurate measurement of the *average* density of artifacts across the collection unit. If survey crews locate dog-leash circles where artifacts are especially dense, they introduce sampling bias that will result in systematic overestimation of densities. In effect, the densities of unusual high-density artifact "hot spots" will be taken as typical. Since artifact densities often do show considerable small-scale variability across collection units, the impact of this bias could be severe. It must be avoided.

One way is to select the locations of dog-leash circles from too far away to see what's on the ground there. Decide, for example, to do a systematic collection "over there to the left of that bush." This amounts to a quick-and-dirty way of randomly selecting a location. Another way could be to look at the ground and decide what a typical density in this collection unit looks like, mentally averaging together high- and low-density areas so as to be sure that whatever location is selected looks like the typical image for the collection unit.

2. Why is it not okay for a survey crew to intentionally locate a dog-leash circle for a systematic collection, so as to be sure to include a figurine head or a greenstone bead or a rare and beautiful very early Neolithic sherd they have spotted? What should they do in such a situation?

Systematic collections offer an especially good opportunity for accurately estimating the ratios of unusual things to more common things like sherds. If dog-leash circles are purposefully located so as to include unusual things, once again a serious sampling bias is introduced. The ratios of those unusual things will be artificially inflated. It is often a good idea to encourage survey crews to collect unusual but informative things even when they don't fall within collection circles, but they should be collected and tagged separately so that they do not become part of the calculation of densities or ratios.

3. Suppose that the basic data-recording units of a survey are collection units 25 x 25 m, each of which is to be sampled with up to four systematic collections in different parts of the collection units (as many as necessary to acquire a specified number of artifacts). Should the coordinates of each systematic collection be recorded by GPS? Why or why not?

A tendency to record coordinates for a lot of things can grow, just because our GPS units make it fairly easy to do it. If several systematic surface collections are made in such a way as to provide an accurate measurement of *average* densities and proportions of things across a collection unit, there is little to be learned from their individual locations separately. Moreover, errors of 5–10 m or more are likely to be associated with measurements in the field by handheld GPS units (manufacturers' specifications notwithstanding). This means that, with collection units 25 x 25 m, the coordinates recorded would provide little better locational information than simply knowing which collection unit the circles were in; indeed, the GPS coordinates would often locate the circles in the *wrong* collection units. It might not take much time to record the coordinates but it really would be wasted time: because it's quick and easy is never a good reason for doing something that's meaningless.

Along similar lines, it is common practice to simply bag together all the artifacts collected in several collection circles designed to provide an average measurement for a single collection unit area (and this does save time, in the field and in the lab). As long as the number of circles is recorded so that the area the artifacts came from is known accurately, no meaningful information is lost by not recording which artifacts came from which circle or where exactly each circle was.

4. What might we do to compensate for the impact of varying vegetation cover on the measurement of artifact densities in different collection units?

It certainly is plausible to think that when vegetation cover is heavy, the lowered surface visibility will depress artifact density measurements. One simple way to assess and combat such effects is to record a subjective rating of vegetation cover as heavy, medium, or light at each collection location. The density values recorded in the different vegetation categories can be compared later. If there are strong and significant differences between the three groups of density values, these differences can be used to calculate a number or a percentage to add to the density measurements made in medium and heavy vegetation to put them on a scale compatible with the measurements made in light vegetation.

This approach does implicitly assume that there is no reason to believe that there is a relationship between vegetation and "true" density values. That is, an approach like this should not be used if there is any suspicion that low-density scatters tend strongly to occur on steeper slopes, which is also where high-density vegetation tends to occur. Under circumstances like these, the low density values recorded in high-vegetation conditions should definitely not be "corrected" to be more compatible with measurements made in light vegetation.

5. Suppose systematic collections in dog-leash circles are used to estimate the overall artifact density in 1 ha collection units where densities are high enough for this to be practical. Where densities are too low for this, could you measure density by dividing the number of artifacts from a general collection across the entire collection unit by the total area of the collection unit?

This way of measuring densities in low-density areas would be a mistake, quite likely of serious proportions. When a circle of 10 m² is marked off and surface collected, the examination is inevitably *much* more intensive than the examination of an area of 1 ha can possibly be. Collecting in dog-leash circles by teams of several people can result in collecting virtually 100% of the artifacts that are present on the surface. Collections made by wandering around in an area of 1 ha will never collect anything approaching 100% of the artifacts present on the surface. The two calculations of density are entirely incompatible.

6. On regional survey why might you decide to collect only ceramics rather than all artifacts?

We have been somewhat vague about exactly what gets collected in the surface collections we have talked about. Sometimes regional surveys collect all artifacts; sometimes they collect only ceramics; sometimes they collect everything except flaked stone. For ceramic-producing societies, ceramics are the most fundamentally useful artifacts to collect. They are usually the most abundant; they provide a good indication of the quantity and nature of garbage disposed of in a place; and they are the most likely artifacts to be chronologically diagnostic (that is, the characteristics of a sherd, all by themselves, can often tell us what period it pertains to).

Flaked stone artifacts can also tell us much about the differences in activities that occurred in different places, and many regional projects have collected them. They are considerably less likely to be chronologically diagnostic than ceramics, however, and that may make it difficult to learn very much from them, since in multi-component occupation areas it may not be possible to determine which component they should be assigned to. Even with training the members of survey teams are likely to have very different abilities to spot flaked stone artifacts on a rocky surface, so recovery rates may be erratic. For reasons like this, some projects have decided not to collect flaked stone. Especially if more detailed and intensive work is anticipated and flaked stone is scarce, it may make more sense to leave it where it is for recovery in a context where more can be learned from it. On the other hand, specific kinds of information about flaked stone from different locations may be vital for answering particular research questions.

In this connection it can be noted that some surveys have been carried out without collecting anything; artifact analysis is simply done in the field, recording quantities of different kinds of material, which is then left where it was found. Doubts have been expressed about whether artifact analysis of this sort is very reliable. It also means that there are no collections to return to later when, say, a more precise ceramic chronology has been established. If there are no collections, however, one escapes the "collections dilemma" of figuring out how to store and maintain the things we collect in the field.

7. In some regions there is reason to worry that low-density artifact scatters do not represent ancient occupations, but only artifacts brought from elsewhere by modern farmers spreading manure or compost in their fields. How could you use the data collected in a regional survey to evaluate this possibility?

Stratigraphic testing or remote sensing, such as magnetometry or ground-penetrating radar, can be used to determine whether in situ structural remains or other features are associated with low-density surface scatters. Short of this, there are likely to be patterns internal to a regional dataset that can help resolve this issue. Spreading of compost or manure is likely to mean collecting these materials in or near villages where they accumulate in quantity and transporting them out to fields. These practices are likely to be most intensive closer to the modern villages that are the source of the materials, so if low-density scatters of ancient materials tend especially to occur close to modern villages, we should be suspicious that those low-density scatters might have been created in this way. Manure or compost brought from modern villages may contain not only ancient sherds from those modern village locations, but also modern sherds and plastic. If the presence of plastic is noted on survey, we can see whether low-density scatters usually correspond to noticeable concentrations of plastic as well. If *all* sherds (including modern ones) are collected, we can investigate whether modern sherds are also especially abundant in low-density scatters of ancient ceramics.

8. It is commonly feared that material of the earlier periods in a sequence is poorly represented in surface collections because it has been covered over by later occupations at the same sites. How could you evaluate the extent to which a survey dataset is affected by this problem?

The stratigraphic principles of accumulation of debris that place newer materials on top of earlier materials are deeply embedded in archaeological education. This makes it seem quite doubtful that early materials can be as well represented as they should be in surface collections, particularly in areas that have long sequences of occupation. Regional survey data based on surface collection can be compared with the results of stratigraphic testing or larger-scale excavations in the same localities to assess the proportional representation of materials of different periods. The obstacle to this sort of comparison is usually that the excavations have already taken place; no collections or other systematic observations were made of surface assemblages beforehand; and the very fact of the excavations has altered the nature of surface assemblages, making comparison of excavation data with surface data collected following the excavations suspect. More systematic observation of sites prior to excavation (and publication of this information) would open the door to interesting methodological exploration.

Any regional survey project that also incorporates at least some stratigraphic testing obviously provides a particularly attractive opportunity for this sort of study. In one example stratigraphic testing at site 374 in the Chifeng region revealed no sign of materials from the two earliest periods in the sequence, both of which had appeared in surface collections made previously, along with much more abundant materials of four later periods. Deposits more than 4 m deep dating to these later periods had not prevented Early Neolithic sherds from working their way to the surface. Surface collection all across a site may well represent sparse materials from very early occupations better than excavated assemblages from a few specific locations within it.

When shovel probes or other means of subsurface testing are part of the regional survey strategy, the results of subsurface testing can be compared with surface collections. If shovel probes are not part of the overall survey strategy, a modest program of shovel testing could be carried out for specific comparison with surface collections. In the Valle de la Plata, comparison of the assemblages from thousands of surface collections and thousands of shovel probes (which were excavated to sterile soil) revealed that materials from the earliest periods were actually very slightly better represented in the surface collections than in the shovel probes.

9. The destruction of archaeological sites by soil erosion and their burial by the deposition of natural sediments on top of them are common concerns. Detailed landscape reconstruction by a qualified geomorphologist can help assess these possibilities. How can further assessment be incorporated into the archaeological survey itself?

Natural processes, especially those attributable to wind and water, are continually modifying the landscapes we study through regional survey. Auger coring is a possibility for dealing with remains we know to be covered over by sediments, but the question here concerns how we can assess the likelihood that such measures may need to be taken in the first place. Simply surveying a region and assuming that the places where we find no evidence of occupation are places where no one lived, begs the question. We may find sites in eroded uplands, but this does not prove that erosion is not an issue; perhaps we should have found more, but many were washed away. We may find no sites on alluvial valley floors and wonder whether they are simply several meters below the present ground surface.

Field survey can be opportunistic in making observations relevant to these issues. In particular, attention to areas where sediments have been deposited—such as alluvial valley floors—is likely to pay off. Especially if survey is finding little evidence of occupation in such areas, special efforts can be made to examine the backdirt from wells and other excavations to see if it contains ancient cultural materials. Modern construction of even modest structures is likely to require excavations up to several meters deep, and large structures require much deeper foundations. Whenever possible such excavations can be explored for buried surfaces, recognizable archaeological features, and artifacts in profiles. Natural erosional gullies can also often provide such opportunities. Conversation with people who live in the region can be highly informative on this score. An abundance of such casual observation without finding buried archaeological remains can suggest that they are not there to be found. It is also possible to quantify such observations and treat them as a sample of the zone subject to risk of buried sites.

Such observations are equally useful in addressing the possibility that erosion has destroyed sites. If water-borne sediments are being deposited in valley floors, those sediments were picked up by water higher in the uplands where erosion is taking place. If artifacts are being removed in the same way, the process does not destroy the artifacts; it just moves them. The artifacts should wind up in the same places as the sediments. These same kinds of observations, then, of areas where sediments are being deposited can be helpful in assessing damage to the regional archaeological record by both erosion and deposition. If artifacts are discovered in these observations, they might be evidence of either buried sites or sites eroded off higher ground. If the artifacts occur in concentrations and in situ features are observed, then the former is indicated. If the artifacts are more widely scattered and occur at a variety of depths from the surface on down, then the latter is a more likely possibility. If artifacts are simply not found in this way, then it is likely that both destruction of sites by erosion and burial of sites by deposition are minimal.

SUGGESTED READINGS

Archaeological Survey by E. B. Banning (Kluwer Academic/Plenum Publishers, New York 2002); *Archaeological Survey* by James M. Collins and Brian Leigh Molyneaux (Altamira Press, Walnut Creek, CA, 2003); and *The Archaeological Survey Manual* by Gregory G. White and Thomas F. King (Left Coast Press, Walnut Creek, CA, 2007). A wide array of practical, technical, and statistical issues are discussed in these three archaeological survey manuals. The latter two are strongly focused on survey in a heritage management context. Overall attention to research questions at the level of human communities and societies is quite limited in all three; attention to demography is almost entirely absent.

"Mapping of the Spatial and Temporal Distribution of Archaeological Sites of Northern China During the Neolithic and Bronze Age" by Mayke Wagner, Pavel Tarasov, Dominic Hosner, Andreas Fleck, Richard Ehrich, Xiaocheng Chen, and Christian Leipe (*Quaternary International* 290–291:344–357, 2013). Argues, contrary to the view expressed in this chapter, that a national cultural heritage inventory can provide a basis for meaningful demographic analysis on a scale of hundreds of thousands of square kilometers.

"Surveys and Mesoamerican Archaeology: The Emerging Macroregional Paradigm" by Andrew K. Balkansky (*Journal of Archaeological Research* 14:53–95, 2006). Argues that new perspectives on social dynamics emerge from amalgamating regional-scale surveys carried out with methodology like that discussed in this book into an integrated view of 10,000 km^2 or more.

Surface Archaeology edited by Alan P. Sullivan III (University of New Mexico Press, Albuquerque, 1998). A collection of papers addressing various aspects of learning from archaeological remains on the surface. Methods for collecting data are addressed but the emphasis is heavily on drawing conclusions about human communities and their activities. The scale of analysis is smaller than the regions this book focuses on.

"The Siteless Survey: A Regional Scale Data Collection Strategy" by Robert C. Dunnell and William S. Dancey (*Advances in Archaeological Method and Theory* 6:267–287, 1983). An influential argument that using sites as fundamental units of data recording and analysis risks missing important information in the field and patterns in analysis. The data collection strategy proposed was mapping all individual artifacts as point locations. The "region" to which the strategy was applied totaled 8 ha.

"Chiefdoms and States in the Yuncheng Basin and the Chifeng Region: A Comparative Analysis of Settlement Systems in North China" by Robert D. Drennan and Xiangming Dai (*Journal of Anthropological Archaeology* 29:455–468, 2010). An effort to compare demographic trajectories for two regions led to an extended consideration of how different approaches to measuring area and density with fundamentally similar objectives yielded incompatible numbers that required special treatment for valid comparison.

Side-by-Side Survey: Comparative Regional Studies in the Mediterranean World edited by Susan E. Alcock and John F. Cherry (Oxbow Books, Oxford, UK, 2004). A good many chapters deal with field methods, mostly considerably more intensive and focused on smaller regions than those discussed in this volume. Sophisticated discussion of how difficult it can be to compare data collected by different field methods. Surveys discussed range in scale up to vast areas in which clearly only the "important" sites are recorded.

"iTrowel: Mobile Devices as Transformative Technology in Archaeological Field Research" by Nathan Goodale, David G. Bailey, Theodore Fondak, and Alissa Nauman (*SAA Archaeological Record*, May 2013, pp. 18–22). An enthusiastic pitch for iPads equipped with GIS software for recording data in archaeological field survey. The focus is on integrating the technology and making it all work.

"No Surprises? The Reliability and Validity of Test Pit Sampling" by Jack D. Nance and Bruce F. Ball (*American Antiquity* 51:457–483, 1986); "Shovel-Test Sampling in Archaeological Survey: Comments on Nance and Ball, and Lightfoot" by Michael J. Shott (*American Antiquity* 54:396–404, 1989). Nance and Ball raise concerns that small sites and sites with low artifact densities may go undetected, but finally judge shovel probes to be practical and reliable—particularly in conjunction with other modes of data recovery. Shott is harshly critical of the use of shovel probes in commenting on the article by Nance and Ball as well as another by Kent Lightfoot. Nance and Ball respond to Shott in the same journal issue.

Statistics for Archaeologists: A Common Sense Approach (2nd edition) by Robert D. Drennan (Springer-Verlag, New York, 2010). The sampling statistics and other statistical tools used in this chapter and elsewhere are discussed at an introductory level and from a perspective compatible with their use here.

The Archaeology of Regions: A Case for Full-Coverage Survey edited by Suzanne K. Fish and Stephen A. Kowalewski (Eliot Werner Publications/ Percheron

Press, Clinton Corners, NY, 2009). The editors and most of the authors present case studies and abstract arguments in favor of complete surveys rather than using sampling. The three chapters by commentators are considerably more sympathetic to the contexts in which sampling can be useful.

"Geoarchaeological Aids in the Investigation of Early Shang Civilization on the Floodplain of the Lower Yellow River, China" by Zhichun Jing, George (Rip) Rapp, Jr., and Tianlin Gao (*World Archaeology* 29:36–50, 1997). Seven field seasons and 7,000 auger cores up to 12 m deep, mostly concentrated in an area of 6 by 6 km. The focus was learning about a Shang city buried under natural sediment, but Neolithic materials were also recovered.

"Survey, Excavation, and Geophysics at Songjiaheba – A Small Bronze Age Site in the Chengdu Plain" by Rowan Flad, Timothy J. Horsley, Jade D'Alpoim Guedes, He Kunyu, Gwen Bennett, Pochan Chen, Li Shuicheng, and Jiang Zhanghua (*Asian Perspectives* 52:119–142, 2013). The focus is on documenting one site buried under sediments with auger coring, but there is also discussion of applying the technique across several hundred square kilometers, mostly in the form of long lines of cores laid out purposefully.

"Geomorphic Analysis of Hohokam Settlement Patterns on Alluvial Fans along the Western Flank of the Tortolita Mountains, Arizona" by Michael R. Waters and John J. Field (*Geoarchaeology* 1:329–345, 1986). Analysis of geomorphology to complement archaeological survey concludes that patterns of Hohokam artifact distribution are attributable mostly to where Hohokam residence and other activities occurred, rather than to patterns of natural erosion and deposition of sediments.

CHAPTER 6

CONCLUSION

We do not consider this book the final word on regional settlement demography in archaeology. We hope that we have made clear why we see demography not as a special perspective some have chosen to adopt in regional settlement analysis, but as the essential foundation upon which regional settlement analysis (very broadly construed in all its aspects) is built. When we look across the past half-century of regional settlement demography in archaeology, we think its methodological growth has been stunted by at least two factors. One is a failure to recognize just how central demography is to all regional settlement analysis. The other is an unnecessary division of those who do pay attention to demography into opposing camps of believers and disbelievers.

Skeptics have raised issues in regional settlement demography that merit discussion; practitioners have not paid as much attention to these issues as we should have. There has been too much preaching to the choir on both sides. Surely it goes without saying by now that we think useful and powerful field and analytical methods for regional demographic analysis have been developed in archaeology. We also underscore that we see much more work to be done in improving these methods. We close, then, by enumerating a few directions we hope will be pursued in the future.

SHARPENING UP RESULTS

The level of precision achieved thus far in archaeological demography is useful, but greater precision would be even more useful. One of the current limitations in this regard is the scarcity of detailed datasets that relate knowledge of excavated structures, features, and stratigraphy to surface remains. Information from site-scale studies—usually involving excavation—is vital to the interpretation of regional-scale data (usually from the surface). Much information is available on excavated sites from many regions, but the persistently missing link is systematic data on the surface remains at those sites before they were excavated. More abundant *published* information of this kind would enable us to make increasingly precise reconstructions of ancient regional demography.

Lack of chronological control also limits the precision of our demographic reconstructions. Shorter periods defined by ceramic styles would obviously be helpful and improvement of this sort will probably occur for some regions. There are, however, well-studied regions where persistent efforts in this direction have not met with success. There may be more hope in new approaches to chronometric dating of ceramics. Thermoluminescence dating is an obvious possibility, although the cost remains very high. Even if the cost can be brought down, it would still be necessary to apply it to collections from regional-scale survey with very sophisticated statistical sampling designs aimed at answering particular kinds of chronological questions.

Comparisons between regions could become sharper with the help of more rigorous mathematical methods for characterizing spatial patterns. Mathematical methods that complement (rather than seek to replace) visual recognition of spatial patterns have particularly great potential. More powerful ways of visualizing spatial distributions that are known only from samples could make sampling a more attractive option in a wider array of circumstances. Methods proposed for analyzing regional archaeological data could be more thoroughly explored and tested with modern settlement and census data, both of which are much more accessible in digital form than they were only a few years ago.

Making Interpretation More Convincing

Regional settlement analyses could take fuller advantage of studying patterns in the archaeological data themselves to assess risks of misinterpretation. This usually springs from explicit recognition of alternative interpretations, as in the example discussed in Chapter 5 of the characteristics we might expect of the spatial distribution of sparse artifact scatters if they resulted from manuring or composting rather than dispersed ancient occupation.

Efforts to pursue different lines of evidence toward the same conclusions could be more vigorous. This is particularly relevant to absolute population estimates. Relying on multiple lines of evidence can put the methods used to make those estimates on a sounder footing, and ex post facto investigation of whether estimates—once made—are consistent with indications from other sources help us determine how much confidence to place in them.

Preserving and Sharing the Data

It is vital that regional survey artifact collections be preserved and made available for further research. They constitute an invaluable sample of artifacts, better representing a region than any other kind of archaeological collection. As such, they can be an unparalleled resource for selecting samples for further archaeometric and other study.

Publication of full, detailed, "raw" data from regional surveys in digital form can facilitate methodological innovation and further research—especially comparative research. Not only can additional and novel analyses be conducted on those published datasets, they can contribute powerfully to the selection of locations for more intensive smaller-scale research—research that can tell us more because the position of those locations in a larger regional-scale context is known. Archaeology has long been familiar with the idea that once an excavation has been carried out, it cannot be repeated because the deposits have been destroyed. Although not themselves destructive, regional-scale surface surveys also cannot usually be repeated because modern construction and other activities will have obliterated at least some of the remains or otherwise rendered wide-ranging survey impossible. The information already collected in regional surveys is all we will ever know about areas of ancient occupation that have subsequently disappeared. It is worth preserving and making available for the future.

SOURCES OF DATA
FOR EXAMPLES

Chifeng International Collaborative Archaeological Research Project. 2011a. *Settlement Patterns in the Chifeng Region.* Center for Comparative Archaeology, University of Pittsburgh.

Chifeng International Collaborative Archaeological Research Project. 2011b. *Chifeng Settlement Dataset.* Comparative Archaeology Database, University of Pittsburgh. URL: http://www.cadb.pitt.edu.

Drager, Dwight L., and Arthur K. Ireland, editors. 1986. *The Seedskadee Project: Remote Sensing in Non-Site Archaeology.* Albuquerque, NM: National Park Service and Salt Lake City, UT: Bureau of Reclamation.

Drennan, Robert D., editor. 2006a. *Prehispanic Chiefdoms in the Valle de la Plata, Volume 5: Regional Settlement Patterns.* Memoirs in Latin American Archaeology No. 16, University of Pittsburgh.

Drennan, Robert D., editor. 2006b. *Valle de la Plata Settlement Dataset.* Comparative Archaeology Database, University of Pittsburgh. URL: http://www.cadb.pitt.edu.

Kowalewski, Stephen A., Gary M. Feinman, Laura Finsten, Richard E. Blanton, and Linda M. Nicholas. 1989. *Monte Albán's Hinterland, Part II.* Memoirs of the Museum of Anthropology No. 23, University of Michigan, Ann Arbor.

Kruschek, Michael H. 2003. *The Evolution of the Bogotá Chiefdom: A Household View.* Unpublished Ph.D. dissertation, Department of Anthropology, University of Pittsburgh.

Liu, Li. 1996. Settlement Patterns, Chiefdom Variability, and the Development of Early States in North China. *Journal of Anthropological Archaeology* 15:237–288.

Parsons, Jeffrey R., Charles M. Hastings, and Ramiro Matos M. 2000. *Prehispanic Settlement Patterns in the Upper Mantaro and Tarma Drainages, Junín, Peru, Volume 1: The Tarma-Chinachaycocha Region, Part 2*. Memoirs of the Museum of Anthropology No. 34, University of Michigan, Ann Arbor.

Peterson, Christian E. 2006. *"Crafting" Hongshan Communities? Household Archaeology in the Chifeng Region of Eastern Inner Mongolia, PRC*. Unpublished Ph.D dissertation, Department of Anthropology, University of Pittsburgh.

Peterson, Christian E., Lu Xueming, Robert D. Drennan, and Zhu Da. 2014a. *Hongshan Regional Organization in the Upper Daling Valley*. Center for Comparative Archaeology, University of Pittsburgh.

Peterson, Christian E., Lu Xueming, Robert D. Drennan, and Zhu Da. 2014b. *Upper Daling Regional Dataset*. Comparative Archaeology Database, University of Pittsburgh. URL: http://www.cadb.pitt.edu.

Schreiber, Katharina J., and Keith W. Kintigh. 1996. A Test of the Relationship Between Site Size and Population. *American Antiquity* 61:573–579.

Wilson, David J. 1988. *Prehispanic Settlement Patterns in the Lower Santa Valley, Peru: A Regional Perspective on the Origins and Development of Complex North Coast Society*. Washington, DC: Smithsonian Institution Press.